JOURNEYBREAD FOR THE SHADOWLANDS

JOURNEYBREAD FOR THE SHADOWLANDS
The Readings for the Rites of the Catechumenate, RCIA

Pamela E. J. Jackson

A Liturgical Press Book

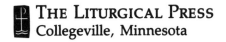
THE LITURGICAL PRESS
Collegeville, Minnesota

Cover design by Greg Becker.

Excerpts from the English translation of *Lectionary for Mass* © 1969, International Committee on English in the Liturgy, Inc. (ICEL); excerpts from the English translation of *Rite of Christian Initiation of Adults* © 1985, ICEL. All rights reserved.

1   2   3   4   5   6   7   8   9

Library of Congress Cataloging-in-Publication Data

Jackson, Pamela E. J.
   Journeybread for the shadowlands : the readings for the rites of
the catechumenate, RCIA / Pamela E.J. Jackson.
        p.   cm.
   ISBN 0-8146-2113-9
   1. Catholic Church.   Ordo initiationis Christianae adultorum.
2. Bible—Study and teaching.   3. Initiation rites—Religious
aspects—Catholic Church.   4. Catechumens—Religious life.
5. Christian education of adults—United States.   I. Title.
BX2045.I55J33   1993
264'.020813—dc20
                                                       92-39442
                                                          CIP

For those who have helped me on the Way

Contents

Introduction

This book began twelve years ago in Aidan Kavanagh's Baptism course at Yale Divinity School, when Father Kavanagh instructed me to read the catechesis and mystagogy of Cyril of Jerusalem, Ambrose, and John Chrysostom in order to find a term-paper topic. I spent much of October Reading Week, 1978, at a picnic table at the foot of West Rock drinking in the powerful preaching that would later provide the main source for my doctoral dissertation. When I reported back to Father Kavanagh, inquiring what he thought I might do with that embarrassment of riches, he suggested I "write a commentary on the new baptismal lectionary." So I did, and after reading it he encouraged me to expand it into a book. I began work on it, but heavy family responsibilities combined with the rigors of working my way, at two jobs, to M.Div. and then Ph.D. continually forced the project to a back burner, until ten years later.

The original paper had explored the relationship between the proper readings of the rites of the catechumenate in the *Rite of Christian Initiation of Adults* and the conversion of those preparing for Baptism. In the decade it lay unfinished, however, years spent learning from Cyril, Ambrose, and Chrysostom greatly deepened my appreciation for the Patristic understanding and use of the Word proclaimed in the worshipping assembly as catalyst for conversion. This use flowed from their experience that (1) the worshipping assembly, being at the heart of the life of the worshipping community, is *ipso facto* at the heart of the conversion process into that community and (2) through the proclamation of the Word in the assembly the Holy Spirit works—in fact, not theory—to draw worshippers into contact with the living God and thereby change them, convert them. Thus, as I returned to expand my original reflections I have sought to root them even more deeply in the Fathers' understanding of the proclamation of the Word in public wor-

1

ship as vehicle through which the Spirit works to effect change from one way of life to another and, thus, as at the heart of conversion.

Contemporary pastoral/liturgical documents have also affirmed both the central role of the worshipping assembly and the power of the Word there proclaimed in transforming the worshippers. Informed by the *Constitution on the Sacred Liturgy*'s understanding of the liturgy as both "summit and source" of the Church's life, the *Rite of Christian Initiation of Adults* expects the various initiatory rites, which will normally be celebrated by a worshipping community (not privately), to play a central role in the process of conversion. The RCIA speaks of the rites as helping the catechumens on their journey, cleansing and strengthening them (nos. 47, 75), leading them into the life of faith, worship, and charity belonging to the People of God (no. 76), and as marking the major, more serious moments of initiation (no. 6). In the RCIA the liturgical seasons shape both the doctrinal formation and the final preparatory period of inward recollection (nos. 16, 75, 81, 138). Specific rites are expected to have particular effects: the scrutinies and presentations are expected to purify minds and hearts, effect repentance and recollection, and impart a deeper knowledge of Christ the Savior; while the scrutinies free from sin and strengthen, the presentations lead to enlightenment and deeper faith (nos. 139, 141, 147). When the General Introduction to the RCIA speaks of the sacraments of initiation freeing men and women from darkness, making them a new creation (nos. 1, 2), bringing them to share in the Paschal Mystery (no. 138), it envisions this as occurring at the Easter Vigil, or at least at a Sunday Mass (no. 127).

It is not only the prayers and ritual actions of the rites which bring about such salutary effects in the worshippers. Conversion comes as response to revelation and "Christ is present in His Word, since it is He Himself who speaks when the holy Scriptures are read in the Church" (CSL 7). Since the proclamation of the Word is thus an integral part of the Church's encounter with the living God in worship, the reading and preaching of Scripture at the rites of the catechumenate are intended to help effect the transformation such encounter inevitably brings. As the introduction to the Lectionary explains,

> The Scriptures, and above all in their liturgical proclamation are a source of life and power. . . . When God's word is proclaimed in the Church and put into practice, it enlightens the faithful through the working of the Holy Spirit and draws them into the entire mystery of the Lord as a reality to be lived. The word of God reverently received moves the heart and its desires toward conversion and toward a life filled with both individual and community faith, since God's word is the sustenance of the Christian life and the source of the prayer of the entire Church (47).

This is why the RCIA calls for special celebrations of the Word to be arranged for the catechumens (nos. 75, 82), and speaks of the Church as nourishing them on the Word of God and sustaining them through liturgical celebrations (no. 47). The RCIA has drawn not only on Patristic structures of initiation (election, scrutinies, etc.), but on the very foundation of those structures: that the Church is born "by water and the Word" not in quaint image but in truth.

The Church at worship is thus at the heart of the conversion process, and this is manifested in the rites of the catechumenate as well as in their Easter culmination. If the celebration of salvation in Baptism and Eucharist is the magnetic north to which the Church is drawn, the locus where the assembly of God's people are most fully who they are created and redeemed to be, then the rites of the catechumenate are a magnetic field radiating outward from the Paschal Vigil; preaching to the converts at the rites of the catechumenate is as crucial to the conversion process as the celebration of the mysteries it draws them to.

None of this is to say, of course, that conversion is limited to hearing the proclamation of Scripture. As the RCIA clearly spells out, there is need for formation in doctrine, prayer, moral life, evangelism, and works of charity, and all of this in the context of being assimilated into the daily life of the Christian community (no. 75). The catechumens themselves may be more consciously aware of God's presence and call in their lives while working with other Christians in a shelter for the homeless or during a meal with a Christian family than they are at a given rite. Yet it is the Word of God that informs the many aspects of conversion, that roots these aspects in Christ, that makes the difference between joining a group of "nice people" or secular altruists, and being grafted into a people who are Jesus Christ dead and risen. If a community is called to teach its catechumens to pray and to obey the Holy Spirit (Introduction 4), how can it do this if its members do not know how to pray or obey the Holy Spirit themselves? And how can they know God well enough to do either if they are not drawing their life from the Word of God, especially as it is proclaimed in the liturgy where "God speaks to His people and Christ is still proclaiming His Gospel" (CSL 33)? Thus, while conversion comprises much more than attendance at preaching, it is not surprising that the first questions asked to determine whether the catechumens qualify for election for Easter Baptism are whether they have listened to the Word of God, and whether they have been true to it.

What I have done in this book, then, is to take the rites of the catechumenate for which there are proper readings (Acceptance into the Order of Catechumens; Election A, B, C; First, Second, and Third Scrutinies; Presentations of the Creed and of the Lord's Prayer; and

Recitation of the Creed), and to explore how each set of readings, in the context of the prayers and ritual actions of its rite, could serve as catalyst for conversion. What images does each reading contain of God, the converts, the Church, through which the Spirit can work to bring catechumens to an understanding of what is happening to them? How does a given set of readings express the conversion experience of the catechumens at a given point on their journey of faith, and how does it work to effect further conversion? How can the Word they hear be incarnated in their lives?

The resulting reflections on the rites are offered here as starting points for meditation for all who are preparing adults for Baptism, or who are seeking deeper conversion themselves. The commentary on each rite is intended to be read slowly, so that readers can stop when something strikes them, and enter into their own reflection on how God might be speaking through these readings to call to deeper conversion. I have tried to explore how the readings, prayers, and ritual actions of each rite describe the experience of conversion, and how they work together to mediate it, as fully as possible, so that sponsors, catechists, and homilists will be able to select from each chapter whatever they find helpful, and use it as a starting point for their own prayer and teaching.

I have provided a source-book for meditation rather than a set of outlines for RCIA preaching for two reasons. First, there are many more occasions for the proclamation of the Word in liturgical celebrations of catechesis than the major rites of the catechumenate which are treated here. The RCIA calls for special celebrations of the Word for catechumens, leaving the choice of Scripture readings to the local community; in addition, the catechumens may well also attend the Liturgy of the Word at daily Mass, being dismissed before the Prayer of the Faithful. Those who enable catechumens to hear God's call to conversion through the liturgical readings thus need to develop their own understanding of *how* God speaks through the proclamation of the Word, since no set of outlines of *what* to say could ever cover all the possible combinations of Scripture readings that could be used.

Second, even in the major rites treated here, the proper Scripture lessons of a given rite can be related to each other in many ways, just as the bright shapes of a kaleidescope can be combined to form a variety of patterns. The task of the preacher is to lift the kaleidescope of the Word to the light of the Spirit, and bring the varied aspects of the lessons to form the pattern best suited to the needs of *these* catechumens and *this* community at *this* specific time. No book could ever take the place of a preacher's own prayerful reflection on the given Scripture lessons in light of a particular pastoral situation, since each conversion is unique and each community has different gifts with which to help its converts. I have thus attempted here to trigger meditation on the readings rather than provide a substitute for it.

A word must be said about the *form* taken by my reflections on the readings of the rites. In my studies of the Fathers I came to share their perception of the Church as living in the world of the Bible in the sense that the Church understands itself in Biblical terms and sees itself as a continuation of the story of God's saving work recorded in the Bible; initiation into such a community therefore includes drawing converts into this Biblical world. As I attempted to reflect on the proper readings of the rites in a way that would show how the proclamation of the Word worked to draw catechumens into the Biblical world, I found that I myself was drawn into the experience of catechumens being drawn into that world. I discovered that the commentary on each reading was being concluded by the final sentence of that reading, as if the commentary were describing the experience of the catechumens "living" the Scripture lesson that was being read, and the repetition of the final sentence was the voice of the lector completing the lesson.

The reflections on each rite, then, need to be read *as if the reader were present at the rite*, witnessing how the Spirit makes the Word proclaimed come to life in the worshipping assembly. The treatment of each rite concludes with a summary section which includes reflection on how the four readings (which were treated individually) relate to each other, and how the readings relate to the ritual actions of the rite and the faith-experience of the catechumens. In addition, there are summary sections following the Rite of Election and the Rites of the Scrutinies and Presentations, which consider the relationship between the proclamation of the Word and the specific stages of the conversion process marked by the rites.

Once my commentary had taken this form, various ways of treating the sets of proper readings suggested themselves, which are presented here not as normative but simply as possible treatments intended to spur readers to develop their own. For example, in considering how the essential content of the Rite of Election might be presented in three different ways using the three sets of propers, it occurred to me that since election initiates a period in which the catechumens are to come to a deeper knowledge of Christ as Savior, the three sets of propers could be treated with varying emphases to depict the salvation He brings from sin (A), death (B), and Satan (C). Similarly, in considering how the three scrutinies instruct the Elect gradually about sin, with the help of the three proper Gospels (no. 143), the proper readings led me to reflect on the ways repentance is necessary in relationship to: trust in

God's providence (I), the way in which human beings perceive things (II), and their response to the Problem of Evil (III); in calling for conversion on ever-deeper levels, the rites of the scrutinies are thus a paradigm of the Christian life. Of course, no flesh-and-blood catechumen will ever live through the proper readings in a way identical to those depicted here. The reflections here, which are based on pastoral experience, are offered to enable readers to perceive how, in their own lives, the Word proclaimed in the worshipping assembly can both express and enable conversion.

What follows, then, is offered simply as one example of what can happen when one gazes into the kaleidescope of the Word, believing it to be catalyst for conversion. Homilists, catechists, and godparents will of course be continually growing in insight from both their own" prayer and their knowledge of their community and catechumens. The purpose of this book is not so much to tell those immediately involved in initiation what to say, as to share the kinds of things that have occurred to one ordinary Christian contemplating the readings in the context of their rites, in the hope of encouraging others pastorally concerned to seek what the Spirit might be saying to them in their own community. These reflections, then, are only what would inform my own preaching to catechumens, based on what I think I would need to hear if I were an adult catechumen—as indeed I was twenty-one years ago.

"There are two ways, one of life and one of death;
and between the two ways there is a great difference."

The Didache

"What the children were seeing may be hard to believe when you read it in print, but it was almost as hard to believe when you saw it happening. The things in the picture were moving. . . . And this was a windy day; but the wind was blowing out of the picture towards them. And suddenly with the wind came the noises—the swishing of the waves and the slap of water against the ship's sides and the creaking and the over-all high, steady roar of air and water. But it was the smell, the wild, briny smell, which really convinced Lucy that she was not dreaming . . .

. . . And by this time either they had grown much smaller or the picture had grown bigger. Eustace tried to pull it off the wall and found himself standing on the frame; in front of him was not glass but real sea, and wind and waves rushing up to the frame as they might to a rock. He lost his head and clutched at the other two who had jumped up beside him. There was a second of struggling and shouting, and just as they thought they had got their balance a great blue roller surged up around them, swept them off their feet, and drew them down into the sea. . ."

The Voyage of the "Dawn Treader"

Prelude

It is a time of threshold, a time of being neither in nor out, a time of seeking the One already found, of being Church and not being Church. The catechumenate is a time of preparation for the consummation of Baptism: a faithful Christian life lived out through time. In the Scripture readings selected for the rites of the catechumenate, the Church communicates to the would-be Christians what it means to be Church, what it means to be catechumen, and who God has revealed Himself to be. The purpose of what follows is to explore the ways in which these readings chosen by the Church help the catechumens to learn to be Church.

Since the Church is a People with a story, the catechumenate is the process of absorbing the catechumens into that story, until the People's story becomes their story, and they are definitely part of its story. Through the Scripture lessons, the catechumens are addressed as Abram, or Peter, or the woman at the well, and come to identify with them; as the catechumens are spoken to as various persons in salvation history, they become part of salvation history. No one, after all, not even the Church, can fully describe conversion, or provide the catechumens with a how-to manual for converting. The Church can only introduce the catechumens to Adam and Noah, to Moses and Martha, who will become their unseen comrades on the journey toward grace.

And journeying is what the catechumenate is about, because the Church understands herself as a People on a journey between then and now—the then of Israel, the then of Jesus, and the now of the local community; through the readings of the ceremonies of the catechumenate, the catechumens—themselves journeying between unbelief and faith—are continually inserted into the history of a People on the move. The journey of the catechumenate is a journey between extremes, be-

Thomas
Merton,
Contempla-
tion in a
World of
Action

tween rebellion and obedience, darkness and light, slavery and sonship, death and life. There are no real maps for this voyage and if
the Church attempted to draw one it would probably end up like "those
curious productions of fourteenth century cartographers which inform
us 'here are many dragons.'" The catechumenate *is* a land of dragons,
and a land where water bursts from rocks, the many-hued promises
of God eerily overarch the terrain, and grace is not cheap. The only
landmarks are the encounters with God of those of the People who have
gone before. As the catechumens attend the Liturgy of the Word during their years of ripening in the faith they will run across a child who
sneezes seven times, elders who can't keep their trees straight, an up-
pity leper, and a suspicious-looking pillar of salt: the catechumenate
is a land of promises and warnings.

The catechumenate is not only a time for learning the stories of faith,
but also for learning the language of faith. After the initial Rite of Acceptance into the Order of Catechumens, virtually the only words which
the catechumens speak in the public rites of the RCIA are the psalm
refrains. Knowing that a child learns language by imitation, the Church
teaches the catechumens the language of the kingdom by allowing them,
with her, to cry for mercy, to trust, to invoke protection, to praise,
to wait. The psalms selected for the rites of the catechumenate often
personalize the Old Testament readings that precede them, articulating the unspoken prayer of the main character in the Old Testament
lesson. The Church cannot provide absolute latitudes and longitudes
for the catechumens on their journey, but she can and does teach them
her songs.

By allowing the catechumens thus to pray with her before the process
of becoming Church is completed in them, the Church witnesses to a
seeming paradox: the readings of the rites of the catechumenate are
addressed to the Church as well as to the catechumens. As the catechumens are coming to a first realization and appropriation of redemption already won, simultaneously, the Church is seeking a fuller
appropriation of redemption, already won and claimed. Now the
Church identifies with John, pointing out the Lamb of God to the
catechumens, now she identifies—with the catechumens—with rebellious Israel. The Church is the Promised Land, but she is also like the
arrow that continually halves the distance between itself and the mark
and never reaches it—on earth. In her struggle for ongoing conversion,
the Church often admonishes her members as if all were catechumens;
yet she is aware that there are stages in the journey and that initial decisions to follow her Lord must be made before deeper decisions are
possible. As the catechumens hear the People addressed as who they
are, or were, or should be, they begin to understand what they are grow-

ing towards. In reestablishing the catechumenate the Church has shown psychological realism: it takes time to grow; in the tension between opposites the catechumens are going through the uncomfortable process of becoming. As they listen to the readings of the rites and are challenged by the same contrasts and opposites challenging those already Church, they gradually become familiar with the geography of the land in which the life of faith is lived.

In studying the readings for the rites of the catechumenate, one might expect each rite to focus on one specific image, and for there to be a progression of imagery from one rite to the next; this is not the case. The richness of Scripture makes it impossible to limit any rite to one particular image, and since some of the rites can be anticipated, any sequence in which the rites are performed will have its own progressions of imagery. The readings contain myriad images of the Church, of God, of the catechumens, but the one overarching icon of the catechumenate is that of the journey between opposite extremes. Each rite presents a unique combination of sets of opposites and articulates the tension between them . . .

I. The Rite of Acceptance into the Order of Catechumens

"The rite that is called the rite of acceptance into the order of catechumens is of the utmost importance. Assembling publicly for the first time, the candidates who have completed the period of the precatechumenate declare their intention to the Church and the Church in turn, carrying out its apostolic mission, accepts them as persons who intend to become its members. God showers his grace on the candidates, since the celebration manifests their desire publicly and marks their reception and first consecration by the Church" (no. 41).

RCIA	Lectionary
nos. 6, 7, 18, 41–74	Ps 34:2, 3, 6, 9, 10, 11, 16
	Gen 12:1-4a
	Ps 33:4-5, 12-13, 18-19, 20, 22
	John 1:35-42

Those who present themselves at this church on this date seeking to be made catechumens are not here by chance. They have already begun to be seduced by a love too shockingly good to be true, except that it is. Somehow they have stumbled across the news that they were created to be totally and perfectly loved, and to reflect this love back to its Source and to all people. Yet they find in themselves things that are opaque to this love they were born to receive and give. Perhaps they have struggled hard to rid themselves of these things, only to discover they cannot; at any rate, at some point someone told them that
John 8:12   the only light bright enough to blot out their darkness is Jesus Christ. They have heard that in Christ they could receive not only forgiveness of sins, but also power to be continually transformed: that Christ the Light would not only make them ever more transparent to the Father's love, but would also, by His Spirit, as with a diamond on glass, etch within them His own image. They would not thereby cease to be themselves, and would, in fact, be more and more their true selves, but the divine love streaming through them would pass through the shape of Christ.

And when at last they asked what they needed to do for such an astonishing metamorphosis to be wrought in them, someone explained that God works it in those who hear and obey His Word. So now they have come to join themselves to a People called together to hear that
RCIA 48   Word and be formed by it. Members of the People meet them outside the main place of worship, and the celebrant, speaking for the community, asks the outsiders who they are, what they ask, and why; they
RCIA 52   ask the Church for faith. Since faith requires a journey, the celebrant
Heb 12:2   asks them if they are ready to follow Christ who is trailblazer of this journey, and asks the community if they will help the new companions on the way to follow Him. The candidates are then signed with
RCIA 54–56   the Cross on their foreheads and senses, reclaiming the means through which they perceive and thus respond for the purpose for which those means were created; to perceive as Christ perceives, and thus be able to act as He acts. The community knows that without a way of seeing and hearing, thinking and speaking, which is irradiated by the Cross, the wayfarers will lose sight of the One who alone can lead them safely to journey's end. They as community learn daily of the Cross's power to change the way one walks by changing the way one perceives and experiences: they join, celebrant and sponsors, in blessing the newcomers with the sign which must now more and more determine their steps.

Now they are prepared for the journey. Now they are numbered among the People who journey, for they have been branded with the sign of contradiction of the One to whom the People belong. Now they

RCIA 60 are catechumens, and they look to the People who are Church to show them where the path of faith begins.

Ps 34:12 R⫽ Come, my children, and listen to me;
I will teach you the fear of the Lord.

I will bless the Lord at all times;
His praise shall continually be in my mouth.
My soul makes its boast in the Lord;
Let the afflicted hear and be glad.
Look to him and be radiant;
So your faces shall never be ashamed.
O taste and see that the Lord is good!
Happy are they who take refuge in him!
O fear the Lord you his saints,
for those who fear him have no want.
The young lions suffer want and hunger;
but those who seek the Lord lack no good thing.
Ps 34:2, 3, 6, The eyes of the Lord are toward the righteous,
9, 10, 11, 16 and his ears toward their cry.

The catechumens have asked the Church for faith, but not just any kind of faith, such as intellectual assent to certain Christian propositions; that kind of faith they already have or they would not be here. They have asked for the faith that will give them eternal life: saving faith. They need the saving knowledge that the good news they have heard is true, not in some distant, abstract sense, but that it is true for them personally—and they need to know what this entails. The Church responds to their asking for this saving faith by inviting them to come and learn the fear of the Lord. The Church has learned from those of the People who have gone before that fear of the Lord is the way to Prov 9:10 approach Him, the beginning of wisdom, the first steps on the path of faith. For to fear the Lord is to perceive and honor God for who God is—the One who made all, knows all, loves all, but whose ways are not ours. To fear the Lord is to abandon false gods cast in the image of one's own desires, for trust in the One who orders all to the greatest good, and obedience to Him. This fear, which is not terror but reverence and awe, finds its ultimate expression in worship, for in worship creatures come before God recognizing who God is and who they are; as this meeting deepens their understanding of the One who Sir 2:18 is infinite majesty and infinite mercy, they praise.

So the Church guides the catechumens in the first steps of their journey by leading them into worship, both by inviting them to join in praising God in the psalm, and by leading them physically to the place of RCIA 60 the worshipping assembly. Soon the Church will draw them further on the way by sharing with them the story of what she has seen on her journey so far. But that story is really God's story; God is the main character, and the telling begins abruptly: "The Lord said." The catechumens need to hear something of what this Lord is like, so they will know how to listen to the story and understand it. The psalm tells them God is good, that He gives good things to those who seek Him, "for those who would draw near to God must believe that He exists and that He rewards those who seek Him." Those who fear the Lord have no want, since to know God for who God is, is to lack nothing. This God looks out for, listens to, those who are seeking Him and is a refuge for them. He is the light the catechumens have been searching for who makes all who look to Him radiant.

Heb 11:6

The catechumens also need some picture of who they are in relationship to this God and of who the Church is, who tells them His story. The psalm images the catechumens as children in the household of faith, and the Church as their teacher, who instructs them in how to relate to God, what it means to fear Him. The Church is presented as proclaiming to the afflicted (perhaps including the catechumens) that God is the only true source of joy, as inviting all to trust in His goodness and experience it, taste it; after the rite the catechumens will be expected "with the help of some of the faithful" to "share their joy and spiritual experiences." Members of the Church are called saints, holy because they belong to a holy God, righteous because they are what He created them to be; they are seekers who cry to God and take refuge in Him. As the catechumens begin to imagine themselves in these words and, by praying them, begin to share in the Church's witness to the afflicted, the words are beginning to be fulfilled in them: they are beginning to be Church.

RCIA 67

Through the processional psalm the Church not only provides the catechumens with images of God, Church, and themselves, but also with the pairs of opposites that serve as points of reference for their journey. The chosen verses contrast the afflicted with those who are glad because their boast is in the Lord; the ashamed, with the radiant; and young lions, who seem invincible but who rely on natural strength and can go hungry, with those seeking the Lord who lack no good thing. The Church also urges the catechumens to learn the truths on which their new life is based; they are exhorted to look, to taste, to learn a fear expressed in trust, obedience, and praise. In the proclamation of the psalm, the Church both illustrates how one praises God, and gives the catechumens an opportunity to learn by doing. As they join in praying the psalm, they are beginning to speak the language of their new People, the language of witness to what God has done, and praise.

"Come my children, and listen to me; I will teach you the fear of the Lord." The fear of the Lord—how to relate to Him—is learned in the Church, the assembly of those who worship; and so the psalm has accompanied the catechumens' being brought into the Church to learn. Their journey has begun, as it will someday end, in praise. They have prayed their first prayer with the Church as part of the Church, and the very act of praying drew them in. Though not yet of the Faithful, they are outsiders no longer, for they have been brought into the locus where the Church meets God. It is in this place—the worshipping assembly—that the Church explains why she praises, by beginning to tell her story. In learning fear of the Lord—to recognize God for who He is—the catechumens' first action was to praise; their second is to listen.

To tell one's story truly is to reveal the heart of one's unique identity, to share the most deeply precious thing one has. It is an act of solemn intimacy. The book from which the Church will tell her story, the book from which the living Word will flash forth and illumine the assembly, is borne in procession to the lectern and honored with incense. The story begins, as all stories, at the beginning:

RCIA 61

> The LORD said to Abram, "Go from your country and your kindred and your father's house to the land I will show you. And I will make of you a great nation, and I will bless you, and make your name great, so that you will be a blessing. I will bless those who bless you, and him who curses you I will curse; and by you all the families of the earth shall bless themselves."
>
> So Abram went, as the LORD had told him.

Gen 12:1-4a

The processional psalm gave instruction on how to relate to God in verbs and adjectives; the Old Testament lesson provides a human model. Abram was one who accepted the invitation to fear the Lord, who learned to trust Him completely and always follow after and praise Him. The Church knows that people become like those they identify with, so she tells of those who have gone before to encourage the catechumens to identify with them, and thus emulate their behavior.

Yet it was not Abram, any more than it was the catechumens, who began the story. It was God who began it by calling Abram in order to draw humankind into a closer relationship with Him. One can only know of this God what He chooses to reveal through His actions. Here He is glimpsed as caller and guider, promiser and rewarder, the All-Powerful who brings great blessing to those who obey. The catechumens are portrayed as summoned to leave all that is familiar—the ways of thinking and acting, the patterns of relationship, which give them security and orientation—for a journey with no itinerary to a destination unnamed. This land the Lord will show them when they get there, this land of promise, is the Church, a great nation called to be a blessing.

What the catechumens have embarked on today is no less than a journey to a new identity; for at its heart conversion is about identity, the journey from the "old man" to the "new." In this rite, the catechumens are committing themselves to leaving a way of life where their goals and the means of obtaining them were determined by self, in order to seek true Life, where their goals and priorities, and the way to them, are determined by God. The catechumens have set out to become who they were created to be, not alone, but as part of a redeemed People. Pulling up stakes and setting off for parts unknown is a wrenching business, involving "human divisions and separations." But what the catechumens have asked for was not to live happily ever after, but faith, and this can only be learned on the journey whose far boundaries are named "your native place" and "the land that I will show you"; it is fitting that their first guide between these extremes is the Father of Faith. To begin, the catechumens are simply summoned with Abram to obey the call to a place the Lord will send them; they are promised God's care, and that they will be blessed. "So Abram went, as the Lord had told him."

Col 3:9-10

RCIA 75

Rom 4:16

Ps 33:12b
Ps 33:22

R/ Happy the people the Lord has chosen to be his own.
     (Lord, let your mercy be on us, as we place our trust in you.)

The Word of the Lord is upright,
   and all his work is done in faithfulness.
He loves righteousness and justice;
   the earth is full of the steadfast love of the Lord.

Blessed is the nation whose God is the Lord,
   the people whom he has chosen as his heritage!
The Lord looks down from heaven,
   he sees all the sons of men.

Behold, the eye of the Lord is on those who fear him,
   on those who hope in his steadfast love,
that he may deliver their soul from death
   and keep them alive in famine.

Our soul waits for the Lord;
   for he is our help and our shield.
Let thy steadfast love, O Lord, be upon us,
   even as we hope in thee.

Ps 33:4-5,
12-13, 18-19,
20, 22,

Worship is a dialogue, and in responding to God's call proclaimed, the Church reaches into the treasure of those before her on the journey, her prayerbook, the Psalter, and shares it with the catechumens. They are told that the God who has called them is faithful and His Word can be trusted, that His love is steadfast and fills the earth. He continually watches out for the People He has called to belong to Him, is their help and protector; He is omniscient and loves what is right. The Church is imaged as a nation blessed to have been chosen as the possession of such a God, a nation who waits for Him and hopes in His love. The catechumens are portrayed as those the Lord has chosen, whom, if they learn the fear of the Lord the Church has offered to teach them, He will rescue from death and sustain in time of need; inasmuch as they learn to wait and hope, trust and ask for mercy, the blessings of the Church will apply to them too. By painting such a detailed picture of what it is like to be part of God's People, the psalm reminds the catechumens that the call and promise they are responding to is made to them as part of a People.

This psalm is an appropriate prayer for the catechumens at the beginning of their relationship with God as part of the Church, because it speaks of the prerequisites of a relationship with Him: being chosen, and deciding to trust Him; it gently informs the newcomers that it is not they who are doing God a favor, but the other way around. It is also appropriate because the catechumens have just heard themselves imaged as Abram, called on a journey to a land far away with no security but the Word of God which promises them blessing. The psalm can be heard as articulating Abram's unspoken response to that call and, thus, as providing the catechumens identified with him with the opportunity to declare with him his and their response. "Happy the people the Lord has chosen to be His own." For thousands of years the People God has called have sung to Him this song of what it means to belong to Him; as today the catechumens join the singing for the first time, they become part of the song.

But now all are standing, and the song has modulated to a new key. For the People know that as much guidance and support as they can offer on the way, it will not be enough to bring the wanderers home. The catechumens must themselves meet the One who breaks the trail; they must see how He walks, so they can recognize His footsteps and follow them to where He waits at journey's end.

℣ We have found the Messiah:

John 1:41, 17b   Jesus Christ, who brings us truth and grace.

John was standing with two of his disciples; and he looked at Jesus as he walked, and said, "Behold, the Lamb of God!"

The two disciples heard him say this, and they followed Jesus. Jesus turned, and saw them following, and said to them, "What do you seek?"

And they said to him, "Rabbi" (which means Teacher), "where are you staying?"

He said to them, "Come and see." They came and saw where he was staying; and they stayed with him that day, for it was about the tenth hour.

One of the two who heard John speak, and followed him, was Andrew, Simon Peter's brother. He first found his brother Simon, and said to him, "We have found the Messiah" (which means Christ).

He brought him to Jesus. Jesus looked at him, and said, "So you are Simon, the son of John? You shall be called Cephas" (which means Peter).

John 1:35-42

In this Gospel the Church continues the process of enabling the catechumens to understand the Christian life and their own experience of conversion through the lens of Scripture by providing them with yet more images of God, the Church, and themselves. God is imaged as in fact God definitively imaged Himself—in Jesus, His Anointed. But the catechumens hear that this Chosen One, who like God is caller and teacher, giver of name and mission, is Himself named as Lamb. In this Gospel, the Church is seen first in the role of John the Baptist pointing Jesus out and revealing His identity to his disciples, among whom the catechumens now count themselves. From the very beginning the Church must be frank that the road to Jerusalem on High the catechumens take up today leads through Golgotha. Those who would follow this Lamb wherever He goes must be told that the altar they seek to stand before they will also end up on; it is so for Him; for them it cannot be otherwise. From the very beginning the catechumens must be put in contact with the Cross, the sword with which the slain Lamb slays; with that emblem they were already marked, and thus identified as set apart to be joined to the one sacrifice acceptable. From the very beginning the Church must be frank that the way to life leads through death, though right now these are only words to the catechumens; they have not yet met Jesus.

Col 1:15

Rev 14:4

Rev 5:6-14

Heb 10:12

"What do you seek?" He asks them. It may still be hard for the catechumens to put it into their own words. Their relationship with God is still more formal than the relationship of intimates. But they want to get to know Jesus and so they ask where He is staying: "Come and see," He answers. To find out what Jesus is like they must follow Him to where He lives, and stay with Him to learn from Him. And here the Church takes on a second role in this Gospel, for the Church is where Jesus is staying, alive in His People; and in this rite the new disciples have followed Him here to learn. As they stay here, they will no longer know Jesus as someone they have only heard about, but as someone they have spent time with and recognize as Messiah. Perhaps they will bring those close to them to meet the One anointed to break all bondage. The Church has well fulfilled her teaching role by introduc-

Matt 23:8 ing them to their true Teacher, who alone understands what it is that each of them needs to know, and will enlighten the ignorance that kills them.

"Jesus looked at him, and said, 'So you are Simon, the son of John? You shall be called Cephas' (which means Peter)." The catechumens have been brought to the One who alone can name them truly, for He knew why He would call each of them into being before all time be-

Rev 2:17 gan. Today they begin to seek that identity for which they were created, in which they will live when time is no more.

Now there is silence. How will they remember it all, the many-dimensioned story into which they have been drawn? How will they get their bearings in this journey's night when they are apart from this

Rev 22:16 assembly, which ever directs their gaze to the Morning Star? And how will they sustain themselves between such feasts on the Word Proclaimed as nourished them today? They need not have worried. The People who have agreed to help the catechumens on their journey share yet one thing more from their provisions. It is the Church's way-bread, which even two millennia has fed her pilgrimage and never will grow

RCIA 64 stale. "Receive the Gospel, the good news of Jesus Christ, the Son of God." Now this book is no longer the exclusive possession of others; now it belongs to them. Now it is no longer to them a closed book, the chronicle of others; from the time the Church opened it to them in the assembly, it has become their history too, and they will find their own story in it.

RCIA 66, 67 Equipped with this treasure, the catechumens are prayed Godspeed, then blessed and sent on the way.

· · · · ·

John Bunyan, This way the new pilgrims have been sent on is, as has been said,
The Pilgrim's a journey between opposite extremes, and the distance between these
Progress extremes is called conversion. The business of the catechumenate is to communicate to the catechumens the essentials they have to know to be able to live their lives as members of the Christian community; the most crucial thing they must learn is how to convert, for Christianity is about converting: about leaving behind a false self for a self ever more deeply conformed to the image of Christ. This is why the catechumenate is rooted in the worshipping assembly, for in the act of worship people are most fully who they are created to be, and thus most open to God and His converting work in them to bring forth their true identity. It would perhaps be easier for the community if the catechumenate could be squeezed into a prefabricated program of

prescribed experiences, if conversion could be parcelled out into various activities, discussion groups, hurdles for the catechumens to clear, and committee meetings, with the rites stuck in for variety as interesting visual aids to illustrate the process. But this would be like thinking a waterfall could reverse its course. The rites of the catechumenate, while they are not training in social ministry or religious education (critical as these are), are in fact the direct link to the source of power for all the dimensions of conversion called for by the RCIA. As the Christian People stand before God in worship, they are transformed into whom God intends them to be; all the aspects of conversion described in RCIA 75 are thus rooted in the worshipping assembly. This means that conversions are not planned by committee, but led by the Holy Spirit, and that priests, catechists, and sponsors are but midwives for a process that ultimately—if it is a genuine conversion—is under the control of Another.

[Relationship of readings to rite and faith-experience]   It also means that the RCIA knows no separation between liturgical rite and faith-experience; the prayers, ritual actions, and Scripture readings of each rite work together both to articulate the catechumens' experience of coming to faith and, simultaneously, to deepen it. The rites are holistic, embracing the affective and physical as well as the conceptual; the ritual gestures of the rites are appropriate to a faith that is not only intellectually, but physically real—as will be indisputably clear on the Last Day. Not only is each rite as a whole inseparable from the catechumens' daily-life experience with the growing pains of conversion, but the individual components (prayers, ritual actions, Scripture) are related both to the converts' experience and to each other. Ritual gestures articulate experience, for example, in the Rite of Acceptance into the Order of Catechumens, as the converts begin to follow the community to saving faith, they physically follow them to the place of worship; as they affirm their desire to belong to the community, they are marked with the community's sign, a gesture suggesting ownership and protection, that they now belong to God in Christ. As the catechumens begin to receive the People's story in the Word Proclaimed, they receive that story in the Book of the Scriptures given to them.

Further, the proper readings of a rite often describe the ritual gestures or prayers of that rite (themselves expressions of inward experience), so that from the very beginning of their initiation, the catechumens are grafted into a community where Word and liturgical action and inward experience of grace are not separate, but inextricably interwoven and continually reflecting on and commenting on each other. In the Rite of Acceptance into the Order of Catechumens, the opening prayer refers to the candidates' decision to become catechumens as entering on a path of faith, setting the scene for the Scriptural presentation of others who left where they were to follow God. The processional psalm proclaims that the Lord's goodness can be tasted—experienced and perceived in His actions—and encourages the catechumens to taste it, immediately after they may have been given salt. The Gospel depicts Jesus as giving His new disciple Simon a new name, shortly after the catechumens may have been given Christian names to reflect their new status as disciples.

This inseparability of rite and faith-experience is especially striking in the Scripture readings. Conversion can be disorienting, an inundation with experiences whose contours are unfamiliar, for which one has no names or categories; the proper lessons enable the catechumens to perceive themselves and what is happening to them in Scriptural terms, and provide them with Scriptural language to articulate it. What the catechumens must learn is how to have a relationship with God, so they need to know what God is like; the best way to find this out is to see how He has acted in the past, and the readings of each rite work together to communicate this. In the Rite of Acceptance into the Order of Catechumens both Old and New Testament lessons illustrate what the psalm explicates: that one seeks to come to God because one has been chosen. Both lessons also make clear that everyone who ever entered into a saving relationship with God was called to leave wherever they were to journey by faith to an unknown place determined by God. Abram is not told where he is going, nor does Jesus answer the disciples' question as to where He is staying. If a place-name would have been no help to Abram because he had never been there and so couldn't imagine what it was like, so it is for the catechumens: one can't imagine what it is like to submit one's life to God, be adopted by Him and indwelt by His Spirit until one is there. And the catechumens can get to a life determined by God only by a road determined by God; the Church can only tell them that fear of Him must be their first step as well as their route, and that this journey is not made alone but as part of a People. The Church can also facilitate the catechumens' socialization into a People that seeks to be surrendered to God by coaching them in the People's patterns of speech. The natural expression of a life centered on God, the native language of His People, is praise of God and His majesty, and the psalms in the Rite of Acceptance into the Order of Catechumens are the perfect primer: they both explain what it means to praise God, and they also express the candidates' entrance into a life of His praise by giving them the opportunity to begin praising Him.

The Scripture lessons of the rites thus provide the catechumens with the framework within which the conversion they are living makes sense, and the words to begin to speak about it. In the Rite of Acceptance into the Order of Catechumens, the converts have heard themselves imaged as children who need to be taught, as summoned into a strange land, as part of a dependent People, as disciples who have only just been called. Already, in one ceremony, the catechumens have been given more word-pictures of their condition than they can remember the next day or exegete as they hear them. Yet the images that may seem to be forgotten have been planted in their unconscious minds, and when, in the time to come, their experience searches for articulation, those images will come to conscious awareness and provide some sense of orientation.

From this time on the Church embraces the catechumens as its own with a mother's love and concern. Joined to the Church, the catechumens are now part of the household of Christ, since the Church nourishes them with the word of God and sustains them by means of liturgical celebrations. The catechumens should be eager, then, to take part in celebrations of the word of God and to receive blessings and other sacramentals. When two catechumens marry or when a catechumen marries an unbaptized person, the appropriate rite is to be used. One who dies during the catechumenate receives a Christian burial.

RCIA 47

II. The Rite of Election

"The second step in Christian initiation is the liturgical rite called both election and the enrollment of names, which closes the period of the catechumenate proper, that is, the lengthy period of formation of the catechumens' minds and hearts. The celebration of the rite of election, which usually coincides with the opening of Lent, also marks the beginning of the period of final, more intense preparation for the sacraments of initiation, during which the elect will be encouraged to follow Christ with greater generosity" (no. 118).

"Before the rite of election is celebrated, the catechumens are expected to have undergone a conversion in mind and in action and to have developed a sufficient acquaintance with Christian teaching as well as a spirit of faith and charity. With deliberate will and an enlightened faith they must have the intention to receive the sacraments of the Church, a resolve they will express publicly in the actual celebration of the rite" (no. 120).

RCIA	Lectionary, First Sunday of Lent		
	A	B	C
nos. 6, 7, 9, 17, 19, 29, 118–137	Gen 2:7-9; 3:1-7	Gen 9:8-15	Deut 26:4-10
	Ps 51:1-2, 3-4ab, 10-11, 12, 15	Ps 25:4-5ab, 6, 7bc, 8-9	Ps 91:1-2, 10-11, 14-15
	Rom 5:12-19	1 Pet 3:18-22	Rom 10:8-13
	Matt 4:1-11	Mark 1:12-15	Luke 4:1-13

The catechumens were last seen some many months ago, resolutely clasping their books and setting their faces for the Celestial City. Unlike Christian's, however, their strengthening by the Word has not been confined to solitary pondering and earnest conversations. The catechumens are journeying with a People among whom the Scriptures are thought of in terms of their proclamation in the worshipping assembly: as the possession not of private exegetes but of the community at worship, in the context of which they came to birth and ever provide a point of access between God and His People. Thus the "special celebrations of the Word of God" held for the catechumens were the fount for their knowledge of Scripture, overflowing into their private study or group discussions, rather than vice versa. Further, the catechetical preaching they heard at these celebrations was not an arbitrarily inserted summary of doctrinal concepts, but an inseparable part of the worship-event, extending the proclamation of the Scriptures outward to draw them in. The worshipping community proclaimed to the catechumens its memory of its encounters with God; as the catechumens absorbed the community's memory, they came to share its identity. And as the catechumens were drawn by this preaching to identify with those before them who encountered God, they themselves were drawn into that encounter. For the purpose of catechetical preaching, and the reason it takes place in the context of the community's encounter with God in worship, is precisely to precipitate that encounter which alone produces the faith that saves.

Learning to meet God in the Word Proclaimed has also been preparing the catechumens to meet Him in the Eucharist, for which they are increasingly hungry, and today have come to ask for. They know that even if they are admitted to the Elect, they are not yet ready for the rich fare of the Faithful; for now, their path to the Upper Room leads through the desert. They turn ever more ravenously to the Word Proclaimed, which they have learned to sustain their lives on, and in the strength of that food they will go forty days and forty nights to the place of tryst.

They have been on the road a long time now. Long enough to know it is not at all what they expected. It has been more wonder-full than they could have dreamed and tougher than they bargained for. They have learned to wrestle to bring every thought captive to Christ, to not be aimless joggers but stoop to bear the weight of others' need, to not be shadow-boxers but gracefully defend themselves from any who would "free" them from the strong embrace of chastity. They have learned to stay on the path even at night, and they have heard a lot of stories. They have discovered that the People whose company they so desired to join are a society not of the sinless but of the forgiven.

John Bunyan, *The Pilgrim's Progress*

RCIA 82

RCIA 75.3

Luke 22:12

1 Kgs 19:8

1 Cor 9:26

2 Cor 10:5

Worse, they have found that the darkness in themselves they seek to eradicate has somehow hopelessly intertwined itself in the very heart of who they think they are. Their illness is not serious, as they had thought; it is mortal, and so is the cure. They are weatherbeaten, their feet have calluses, and they know a lot of songs. They are ready to drown their death in flame and taste the banquet of another world. They are ready for the final stage of the journey, and so they have come back to the assembly to seek permission and provision.

The Rite of Election takes place on the first Sunday of Lent, with the proper readings for Year A, B, or C. The Church does not need to select a special set of propers for the catechumens today. The courtship is ending in betrothal, the wedding is not far off, it is time for all possible candor. The catechumens will soon be one Body with the Faithful, so they must be allowed to hear what God is saying to them; God's Word to the Faithful is also His Word to them. . .

(Year A)   The Faithful do not try to euphemize their condition. "Left to ourselves, here is who we really are," they say to the catechumens, "We are the same as you." The catechumens, as all the Church, know that an affliction hidden for shame cannot heal; they watch solemnly as their common wound is exposed to the light and probed.

> The Lord God formed man of dust from the ground, and breathed into his nostrils the breath of life; and man became a living being. And the Lord God planted a garden in Eden, in the East; and there he put the man whom he had formed. And out of the ground the Lord God made to grow every tree that is pleasant to the sight and good for food, the tree of life also in the midst of the garden, and the tree of the knowledge of good and evil.
>
> Now the serpent was more subtle than any other wild creature that the Lord God had made. He said to the woman, "Did God say, 'You shall not eat of any tree of the garden'?"
>
> And the woman said to the serpent, "We may eat of the fruit of the trees of the garden; but God said, 'You shall not eat of the fruit of the tree which is in the midst of the garden, neither shall you touch it, lest you die.'" But the serpent said to the woman, "You will not die. For God knows that when you eat of it your eyes will be opened, and you will be like God, knowing good and evil."
>
> So when the woman saw that the tree was good for food, and that it was a delight to the eyes, and that the tree was to be desired to make one wise, she took of its fruit and ate; and she also gave some to her husband, and he ate. Then the eyes of both were opened, and they knew that they were naked; and they sewed fig leaves together and made themselves aprons.

Gen 2:7-9;
3:1-7

The catechumens have heard previously that God is Creator and Author of life; they know that as world-maker He constructed the principles by which His world would function, that He determines good and evil. Now they hear that in fact He is a gardener, who plants everything that is beautiful and nourishing to supply all needs. But this life-giving Gardener is challenged by a lying serpent, whose lies are logical, who pretends concern for human good to lure creatures into disobedience to their Creator and automatic self-destruction.

They almost do not need to hear the dialogue. It has been recapitulated in their own lives so many times, they practically know it by heart: Smoothly the thought insinuates itself that if only they had something God has withheld from them, they would be better off. The idea has such a fascinating quality as it slithers through their minds that they are distracted from its implications: that God does not have their best interest at heart, that *they* should determine what is good for them— should, in fact, be God—and that God has lied to them in telling them that to try to be other than He has created them to be is death. Caught up in the attractive coils of imagining how much better things would be for them if they were final arbiters of their destiny, they do not see the obvious: they are only alive because God breathed into them a life of trust and gratitude; to breathe instead the fumes of self-worship is automatically to suffocate and die.

The taproot of their darkness lies exposed at last. They have abandoned the Truth—trust in God's ordering of Creation in the way most loving for all, including them—for the delusion that they are at the center of the universe, that all that is should be ordered to what *they* think is desirable for them. How insane it is, the catechumens see, that the heap of dust they are, animated only by the breath of their Creator, should refuse to trust the One who strung them together from an odd collection of elements from His periodic table. But they have accepted the delusion that their judgement is more trustworthy than God's, and having accepted it the first thing that they do is to spread it, and it becomes pandemic. They have believed lies about the Truth and eaten the fruit of lies, and once they have digested it they show the symptoms of further delusion: They discover yet more things they need that their Creator has not provided, and set about to make up the lack themselves; they realize that the Creator who did not take proper care of them will be angry that they took for themselves what He withheld, and so they hide. They have eaten the fruit of lies and now find themselves paralyzed, incapable of the trust for which they are created, alienated from their true nature; since they have made themselves incapable of doing what alone will fulfill them, it will not be long before, like petty despots, they make war for things that can never satisfy

Hos 10:13

them. Now the catechumens understand why they have sometimes felt somehow not quite at home. They were created to be garden dwellers, but chose to live instead in a slum polluted by the toxic waste of their desire for domination. They have eaten the fruit of lies and die poisoned at their own hand.

The catechumens with the Faithful have seen their ultimate condition before God laid bare: they are sinners who have no excuse. All in the assembly recognize in their own lives the symptoms of eating the fruit of lies; all see they are naked. "And they sewed fig leaves together and made themselves aprons." The catechumens become aware that the lector has been holding up for them a perfect mirror; for the first time they see themselves as they truly are, the mire of the rebellion which clings to them illumined by the eerie glow of a flaming sword.

Gen 3:24

Ps 51:1a

℟ Be merciful, O Lord, for we have sinned.

> Have mercy on me, O God,
>> according to thy steadfast love;
>> according to thy abundant mercy blot out my transgressions.
> Wash me thoroughly from my iniquity,
>> and cleanse me from my sin!
>
> For I know my transgressions,
>> and my sin is ever before me.
> Against thee, thee only, have I sinned,
>> and done that which is evil in thy sight.
>
> Create in me a clean heart, O God,
>> and put a new and right spirit within me.
> Cast me not away from thy presence,
>> and take not thy holy Spirit from me.
>
> Restore to me the joy of thy salvation,
>> and uphold me with a willing spirit.
> O Lord, open thou my lips,
>> and my mouth shall show forth thy praise.

Ps 51:1-2,
3-4ab, 10-11,
12, 15

For those who have participated in the tragedy in the Garden, the *Miserere* is the most appropriate response, and so the Church now teaches her Lenten prayer par excellence to the catechumens; she has only led them into conviction for sin to enable them to cry with her for mercy. They are reassured to hear that despite their perfidy God is still true to Himself. His love is steadfast, His mercy abundant; He can blot out transgression, cleanse and give a new heart and spirit free from sin. He upholds His People, gives and even restores the salvation that brings joy, and it is He who makes it possible for His People to praise Him. Now that her family secret has been shared, the Church admits in praying the psalm that she too can fall, but nevertheless desires not to be banished forever but to be in the presence of God and praise Him. The catechumens confess, perhaps more deeply than before, that they know they have sinned—not just told occasional white lies to acquaintances—they have sinned against God, chosen their selfish love of themselves over His Self-giving love for them, preferred their judgement or convenience to His loving command. They cannot deny they have left the path; their stray footprints confront them on all sides.

After all, that is why they are here today: to acknowledge that the delusion they accepted in the Garden has led them to wallow in filth and they are sick of the stench. They are here today to ask publicly to be washed from their rebellion, and to have a new spirit breathed into them which will help them not to rebel again, God's Spirit, which is Holy. They ask to be stripped of the aprons of disobedience they have placed between themselves and God, and to be restored to His presence, clothed in the salvation He will give them, with the breath to sing joyful praise.

As always, the catechumens find their journey is between opposite extremes: sin and salvation, being apart from God and the presence of His Spirit, stain and the cleanness that comes from washing. Now they have joined Adam and Eve, and all who wander exiled from the Garden, in uncovering their wound and asking for the one balm that can heal it. "Be merciful, O Lord, for we have sinned." All await the Healer's response.

As sin came into the world through one man and death through sin, and so death spread to all men because all men sinned—sin indeed was in the world before the law was given, but sin is not counted where there is no law. Yet death reigned from Adam to Moses, even over those whose sins were not like the transgression of Adam, who was a type of the one who was to come.

But the free gift is not like the trespass. For if many died through one man's trespass, much more have the grace of God and the free gift in the grace of that one man Jesus Christ abounded for many. And the free gift is not like the effect of that one man's sin. For the judgment following one trespass brought condemnation, but the free gift following many trespasses brings justification. If, because of one man's trespass, death reigned through that one man, much more will those who receive the abundance of grace and the free gift of righteousness reign in life through the one man Jesus Christ.

Then as one man's trespass led to condemnation for all men, so one man's act of righteousness leads to acquittal and life for all men. For as by one man's disobedience many were made sinners, so by one man's obedience many will be made righteous.

Rom 5:12-19

The surgeon's knife, honed on the rock of Golgotha, cuts swift and sure, revealing the depth of the wound and what must be done to close it cleanly. If the first reading provided the catechumens with a visual representation of their condition, the epistle gives them a technical diagnosis with prescription for the cure. Once again the catechumens hear that they are under judgement, condemned to death for sin. Yet the Justice before whom they stand condemned as unjust now offers—as free gift—to make them just; He offers to exchange their disobedience for the obedience of His Christ, who will make them righteous and redeem their death for life.

The catechumens find they have lost their bearings in the midst of paradox; as always they are surrounded by opposite extremes: disobedience and obedience; trespass and the grace of God, free gift; condemnation and justification; death and life. The Church tries to explain; one contrast subsumes the rest and towers over all. Their parents, in Matt 7:13-14 forsaking the narrow way of trust to break their own broad path, fell into the gorge of disobedience, but found its steep and craggy walls impossible to scale, themselves and their children trapped in death for leaving the one road that leads to life. Another of their kind set on that road did not trespass, but planting His feet firmly on the path of trust, stretched out obedient arms to draw His own to His righteousness and restore them to the way of life. "The choice is clear," say the Faithful: "the death sentence of disobedience, or life in the graceful embrace of Christ's obedience. The one is not like the other; which would you have?"

The Faithful have already made their choice; they are the "many" for whom grace has abounded, who have accepted the righteousness offered them and are thereby acquitted. They invite the catechumens, through the prayer of the psalm and the instruction of the epistle, to join them in forsaking the behavior depicted in the first reading for the behavior of Christ they will soon see in the Gospel. "With Christ as your righteousness," they proclaim, "with us you can escape serving death as monarch, and reign in life through Christ."

The catechumens begin to understand. When in the Garden their parents refused to trust, they pronounced a fundamental No in the consciousness of their race, which resounded unceasingly throughout the generations. All would be born with its ringing in their ears, until one Luke 1:38 kept from its clamor spoke with her life a Yes, proleptic echo of that Perfect Yes, which was its fruit and source. For in a second garden, Luke 22:42 One of their own pronounced that Yes which silenced No forever, and John 20:15 in a third as Gardener met them to make His Yes their own. "For as by one man's disobedience, many were made sinners, so by one man's obedience many will be made righteous."

The catechumens are relieved. The first reading has described the problem, the psalm cried for an answer, the epistle gave the explanation of the answer. What good news could be left, they wonder, as they stand to greet the Gospel. But now they catch their breath at the vivid colors of the triptych the Gospel reader unfolds before them. It is the icon of the answer.

Matt 4:4b

℣ Man does not live on bread alone,
  but on every word that comes from the mouth of God.

Jesus was led up by the Spirit into the wilderness to be tempted by the devil. And he fasted forty days and forty nights, and afterward he was hungry. And the tempter came and said to him, "If you are the Son of God, command these stones to become loaves of bread."

But he answered, "It is written, 'Man shall not live on bread alone but on every word that proceeds from the mouth of God.'"

Then the devil took him to the holy city, and set him on the pinnacle of the temple, and said to him, "If you are the Son of God, throw yourself down, for it is written, 'He will give his angels charge of you,' and 'On their hands they will bear you up, lest you strike your foot against a stone.'"

Jesus said to him, "Again it is written, 'You shall not tempt the Lord your God.'"

Again the devil took him to a very high mountain, and showed him all the kingdoms of the world and the glory of them; and he said to him, "All these I will give you, if you will fall down and worship me."

Then Jesus said to him, "Begone, Satan! for it is written, "You shall worship the Lord your God, and Him only shall you serve.'"

Then the devil left him, and behold, angels came, and ministered to
Matt 4:1-11   him.

1 Cor 15:22, 45

Salve Regina

Just when they thought that they could return to the Garden, the catechumens find themselves in the desert. It is one thing to hear St. Paul explain the answer to their problem; it is another for them to learn to live it. It is one thing for the catechumens to hear that the New Adam reversed the trespass of the Old by His obedience; it is another for them, poor banished children of Eve, to be rid of the delusion that they are at the center of the universe which ever leads them to trespass from the way. Now they must follow their forerunner to the arena where He trained to change their No into His Yes; they must be led with Him into the wilderness to be tempted, fast with Him for forty days and be hungry. By watching Him they must learn to wrestle with the lying Tempter, so that when in six weeks' time the delusion is washed from their minds, they will not let the Tempter deceive them into inviting it back. The match begins.

The ever-vigilant Deceiver notices that fasting has made their Champion hungry, so he seeks a quick replay of his previous victory. "Your Gardener has led you into the wilderness where there is nothing to eat," he points out; "if only you had what He is not providing, you would be better off." The conclusion is so reasonable. "You're the one who's best qualified to be deciding what you need; why don't you take matters into your own hands? Whatever purpose He created these stones for can't be as important as your needs; why don't you change them into something that will serve a different purpose—use them to satisfy your hunger?" But fasting has left the Champion alert as well as hungry. "The Gardener who planted the Garden and placed my kinsfolk there determines what we need and what food will nourish us. He has told my people that bread is not the only thing by which He sustains our life. He who created all by His Word can sustain us by every Word He speaks. I will not refuse to trust Him. I will not eat the fruit of lies or taste the bread of disobedience. I will entrust my survival to feeding on His Word."

Undeterred, the Deceiver recovers quickly and aims his next move at the Champion's apparent area of vulnerability. "So you want to be guided by His Word," he continues smoothly; "see how He has promised you will be loved, and cared for by angels. Here you are on the pinnacle of the place where He is worshipped, where all His worshippers can see you. Why don't you throw yourself down and give Him a chance to show He keeps His Word to those who worship Him? Give Him a chance to show that He really loves you as He says, and give His people a chance to see it so they can believe in you and love you, and you can be a success in your mission." But the Champion again escapes his grasp. "He who speaks the Word of Promise is the One who determines when and how it will be fulfilled. To try to make Him prove the truth of His promise is not to trust His Word is true. But I trust His Word; I do not need to test it. His promise of love to me gives me my worth; it is all I need. I will not seek to base my worth on love I obtain through striving. I will not seek to find my worth in a 'successful mission' other than the one my Father gives; and any mission built on disobedience cannot succeed in the end. I trust in His love; I will not try to earn it, or test it to prove it, or try to make Him give it to me on my terms. You may quote the syllables of Scripture, but I know the meaning of His Word, and I will obey it. I will not refuse to trust; I will not tempt Him."

The Deceiver abandons his strategy of trick moves, and leaps upon the Champion in the full strength of his fury, throttling Him and throwing Him to the ground. "Trust!" he hisses. "What is trust? An ephemeral nothing! Can you see it, or hear it, or feel it, or smell it, or taste it?

Can you base your life on an insubstantial wisp, more fragile than a cobweb, too frail to bear the weight of the smallest insect? What kind of shield is this trust from those who would dominate you and your kind to your ill? Your race cannot bear to be dominated by any—their blood runs in your veins—how can you leave yourself and them so vulnerable? Your grand schemes to help them are ever doomed—what is this phantom, trust, against an army? Here, see, *here* is reality: all the bright kingdoms that there are, their jostling people, their sounds and smells, the colors of their wealth; you could control them all for their own good. Do with them what you will—just worship me."

This has been the real issue all along and they both know it. Who is to be worshipped? Who is at the center of the universe? What is of greater worth than anything else, from which everything of lesser value derives its worth? Is it God (even when God does not make sense), or is it something—anything—else? The Champion strains under the Deceiver's grip, for He is like His kind; while their No is not encoded in His brain cells He can hear it as a possibility: . . . All these kinsfolk of His, breathing and eating and sleeping and dragging out their days crushed under the Destroyer's cruel reign. Wouldn't anything be justified if only to free them from this bondage? He would be a good governor of those entrusted to Him . . . The word "entrusted" saves Him from the stranglehold, reminding Him no regent for the author of death has power to give life. No king anointed by any save the Ruler of All Heb 2:17-18; can liberate these vassals from their bondage. The Champion is like 4:15 His kind in all respects, save one. "Power is not what makes me who I am," He cries; "obedience gives me my identity. God alone has worth over all, is to be worshipped over all. God only will I serve. Begone!" The catechumens stare openmouthed as the Deceiver slinks away and the angels God had promised indeed arrive to minister.

The catechumens have, of course, long since learned to conquer temptation to obvious evil; in their final training period they must learn the more advanced skill of defeating temptation to apparent goods not willed by God. What is at stake for them in this contest is precisely what was at stake for their first parents: whom they accept as center of the universe and arbiter of good and evil. Their ultimate allegiance must not be even to "what is good" but to the God who determines what is good. Even if they are trying not to displease God but are still setting themselves up as arbiters of what is good, and thus of what course they will follow, they are not really trusting God, and are still succumbing to the delusion that they are the center of the universe. They must wrestle with this consuming desire to instruct God on how to run the cosmos with themselves at the center; they must put it to death and learn to want what God wants, and base their lives on that.

As they wrestle they will discover with chagrin what their true priorities are, to what extent God is what they treasure over all, and how much of their treasure is laid up in material possessions, relationships, prestige, and power. While any of these things received as gift can be a vehicle for God's reign, they cannot be treasured instead of God, cannot be grasped and hoarded as basis for ultimate worth or security. The catechumens must base their security and worth on God, must let what God wants be their treasure, or they will find they have consigned their locked-up hearts to moth, rust, and thief. Further, as the Gospel also points out, they must move from critiquing God's promises by their own evaluation and experience of what is good for them, to allowing their perception to be critiqued by the Word of God.

Matt 6:19-21

Their wrestling match will be arduous and painful and can only be won because of the example and help of the Champion who coaches them. He is not unable to sympathize with their weakness since He has been tested in every respect as they are, though He did not succumb; "because He himself has suffered and been tempted, He is able to help those who are tempted." In the three panels that comprise the triptych of the Gospel, the catechumens have witnessed His assault by the same threefold temptation confronting them to value material security, self-proved worth, and power over trust in God, and have observed how He conquered. They have watched His moves; they must learn His techniques. They have been told again that they must let God's Word be their food if they are to have strength to prevail. But it is not enough for them to have a vague familiarity with the words of Scripture; they have discovered the alarming fact that their Adversary knows them too. They have been warned about the incredible subtlety of evil, how the Deceiver pretends to be concerned with human good only to lead humankind to self-destruction, how he can cite the Scriptures to pass himself off as an angel of light. Long ago the catechumens had heard that the sword of the Spirit given them to ward off their Adversary was the Word of God; today they are relieved they are among a community of warriors who can teach them how to wield it correctly if the Deceiver seek to turn it against them.

Heb 4:15;
2:18

2 Cor 11:14
Eph 6:17

As the Gospel triptych came alive for the catechumens it provided them with arresting images of its central figures. They saw God as one who speaks words that are life-giving food, but who must not be put to the test, and who alone is to be worshipped and served. With the picture of how the Old Adam was tempted by evil and fell still fresh in their minds, they watched how the New was put to the same trial and emerged as victor; they have perceived through this how the "old man" they are journeying away from responds to temptation and how the "new man" they are moving towards does. Above all, they have

[Relationship
of readings
to each
other]

Col 3:9-10

been confronted with the struggle they must carry on these forty days to choose God as what is of greatest worth in their lives, as the center of the universe, to whom alone they will bow down and worship. They must enter into their Champion's word of power: "Begone Satan, for it is written, 'You shall worship the Lord your God, and Him only shall you serve.'" In the readings taken together, both the reality of evil and the picture of true humanity created in the image of God and restored through Jesus have been starkly presented; both what it means to be deceived and under the power of sin, and what it means to be an obedient son have been vividly portrayed. The catechumens have been showed the parameters of their Lenten journey. "Then the devil left Him, and behold, angels came, and ministered to Him." At this point the catechumens have had enough of the lying Destroyer for one day. As their sponsors come to present them for enrollment, they indeed seem like ministering angels.

In the psalm the catechumens prayed to be washed from their guilt; now they will seal the prayer of their lips with the action of the rite, the enrollment of their names. But first the People must make sure those who seek election are strong enough to enter the lists for the desert con-

RCIA 131B test ahead for all. Have they listened to the Word as it was proclaimed? Have they walked by it and thus stayed on faith's journey's path? Have they sought the companionship of their guides on the way, have they prayed with them in the assembly that constitutes them as who they are?

The sponsors have given their consent; now the catechumens are asked for theirs. Do you wish to abandon your delusion that you should be final judge of good and evil, and live instead in the shade of the

1 Pet 2:24 only Tree which makes one wise? "Since you have already heard the
RCIA 132 call of Christ, you must now express your response to that call clearly and in the presence of the whole Church. Therefore, do you wish to enter fully into the life of the Church through the sacraments of Baptism, Confirmation, and the Eucharist?" The catechumens know that they are signing the death warrant for their flesh; they know they will

Gal 2:20, be crucified with Christ. They think of the joy set before them. "We
Heb 12:2 do," they say.

The names of the Elect are proclaimed, and, as always, the Faithful
RCIA 134, provision them by their prayer, this time requesting for them the spe-
135 cial equipment they will need to run with perseverance the race now
Heb 12:1 set before them. "My dear Elect, you have set out with us on the road that leads to the glory of Easter. Christ will be your way, your truth,
RCIA 136A and your life. Until we meet again for the scrutinies, walk always in his peace."

As they gird themselves for the final stages of their journey, the newly Elect know they are not alone; those whose shame they were born with, whose glory they will inherit, will be ever at their side. The Elect depart. Having begun this day by owning their banishment from the tree of life, in forty days they will return to feast upon its fruit.

(see above,
pp. 26–27)

(Year B)

. . . God's Word to the Faithful is also His Word to them. . . .

And the catechumens are eager to hear that Word today, hoping it will speak to their predicament: for their journey has brought into their view black waters from which they can see no escape. Most of them had not gazed into the depths of these waters before they became catechumens, for before they began this pilgrimage, they had not paid much attention to where they were going. They had not spent many hours silently studying the horizon, sharpening their distance vision, considering what lay ahead. In fact, like most of their race they had daily exhausted most of their energy trying to keep from their conscious awareness the only future event of their life that was certain: its end. Now their months on the journey of the catechumenate have provided them with the solitary times of prayer to scan the horizon, and the support of fellow pilgrims to face what they have begun to see there: the horror of death, and its inevitability. And as they have contemplated death's dark waters they have also sought to fathom their source, and traced it, with eyes newly keen from keeping watch on the journey, to their own hearts.

For by now the catechumens have become aware of what the Faithful have known for some time: from deep within them courses the conviction that they are rightful rulers of reality, an irresistable undertow, pulling them to their death. They were fashioned, they now see, to breathe the Spirit of Truth, to draw life from loving service; instead they seek life's inspiration in this current of delusion that they must dominate, even if by violence. They spurn the Breath of Life and inhale the waters of destruction, yet to abandon love as life-breath is to die. When they discover they are drowning, they push others under and stand on them to buy themselves more time. But it is no use. Wherever they look there is no end to these black waters; choking on their refusal to love, they see whatever they do, it will end in death.

What answer do the Faithful have to this? Is the One they honor sovereign over death as well as life? As the reader mounts the ambo, all look to him as to a lighthouse keeper unshuttering the beacon that will show them whether there is hope of rescue:

> God said to Noah and to his sons with him, "Behold, I establish my covenant with you and your descendents after you, and with every living creature that is with you, the birds, the cattle and every beast of the earth with you, as many as came out of the ark. I establish my covenant with you, that never again shall all flesh be cut off by the waters of a flood, and never again shall there be a flood to destroy the earth." And God said, "This is the sign of the covenant which I make between me and you and every living creature that is with you, for all future genera-

tions: I set my bow in the cloud, and it shall be a sign of the covenant between me and the earth. When I bring clouds over the earth and the bow is seen in the clouds, I will remember my covenant which is between me and you and every living creature of all flesh; and the waters shall never again become a flood to destroy all flesh."

Gen 9:8-15

The Word's bright beam reveals more than they hoped for: By their own choice they founder in the torrents of destruction, yet the waters' Lord reveals Himself as One who rescues from the waves of death. But there is more—this One whose majesty looms over all, Himself seeks a relationship with them, and speaks to them a pledge of faithful love. His name is not Destroyer; He is Maker of Promise, and Maker of Covenant, and Giver of Sign of Faithfulness. The catechumens now perceive that the people around them are those who have gone through the Flood and come out alive, who have heard God's offer of covenant and accepted it. Now, in turn, these descendents of Noah make this covenant known to the catechumens, to invite them to join in their bond of commitment with the One who cares for all that lives. The catechumens try to conceive of a God whose answer to their self-invoked deluge in death would be a promise of life and relationship of love. What could such a God be like, they wonder. How would He behave toward those He rescues? What words would one address to Him? And while they are yet flailing in their black maelstrom of rebellion, the catechumens see stretching down to them a many-colored lifeline. "And the waters shall never again become a flood to destroy all flesh."

Ps 25:10

R⁊ Your ways, O Lord, are love and truth,
    to those who keep your covenant.

Make me to know thy ways, O Lord;
    teach me thy paths.
Lead me in thy truth, and teach me,
    for thou art the God of my salvation.

Be mindful of thy mercy, O Lord, and of thy steadfast love,
    for they have been from of old.
According to thy steadfast love remember me,
    for thy goodness sake, O Lord!

Good and upright is the Lord;
    therefore he instructs sinners in the way.
He leads the humble in what is right,
Ps 25:4-5ab,   and teaches the humble his way.
6, 7bc, 8-9

With Noah and his family the catechumens sing to the God who gives them salvation, who has loved them steadfastly from the beginning. He is good, He behaves toward His own in truth, He is merciful forever. He is teacher of sinners and the lowly, leading them to what is right. The heirs of Noah share their song with the catechumens to show them how those who had fatally innundated themselves in delusion address the One who delivered them from death, what He is like, and what it is like to keep His covenant. Though rescued, they recognize themselves as sinners still, as people of many needs: the need for mercy, the need to be led, the need to learn ever more fully how to keep His covenant.

The catechumens can only enter into this covenant if they trust the One who offers it, so the Faithful lead them in their song of trust to enable them to trust more deeply; as the catechumens join in this song, their proclamation draws them further into the trust the rescued have in the God who always remembers His own. The catechumens must come to recognize this God for who He is—the God of their salvation— and seek to follow Him in all. Now as sinners they ask for instruction, for humility, for the grace to be obedient to the covenant, so they may know God's love. As they come to seek election, they proclaim His faithfulness, and pray for their own.

"Your ways, O Lord, are love and truth, to those who keep your covenant." But what is it that will make it possible for the catechumens to join with these heirs of Noah and keep the covenant? For they are still drowning in desire for domination, still self-deluged in death. What is this ark of life which rescues the Faithful from their tempestuous disobedience to love? Who captains it—will he pilot it toward them?

> Christ died for sins once for all, the righteous for the unrighteous, that he might bring us to God, being put to death in the flesh but made alive in the spirit; in which he went and preached to the spirits in prison, who formerly did not obey, when God's patience waited in the days of Noah, during the building of the ark, in which a few, that is, eight persons, were saved through water. Baptism, which corresponds to this, now saves you, not as a removal of dirt from the body but as an appeal to God for a clear conscience, through the resurrection of Jesus Christ, who has gone into heaven and is at the right hand of God, with angels, authorities and powers subject to him.

1 Pet 3:18-22

As their vision becomes more accustomed to the brilliance of the Word, the catechumens can now perceive the means of deliverance from their disobedience: The Maker of All has become a carpenter, and fashioned a rescue ship from the wood of His obedience; on the frame of His faithful death, He has constructed an ark of life. Baptism is this vessel of His righteousness, and, now raised up, its Builder captains it to salvage the unrighteous by His rising. Those whom the Captain of Salvation takes aboard, He calls His Church, and enlists their aid

Heb 2:10

Matt 4:19,   in fishing out more lost. The powers of death shall not prevail against
16:18   this crew, for they bear the number of the Resurrection. To those en-
gulfed in death's black nothingness they cry: "Come to Him whose
bright obedience reaches out to encircle you with the infinite hues of
His divine compassion! Let Him hold you in that rainbow of His arms.
Then, when the One who could by right unleash the torrents of destruction, gazes on the dark rebellion of your sin, He will see it in the
light of that irridescent embrace. He will remember His covenant; you
shall drown no more."

As the catechumens hear the Faithful hailing them with the Word
of their rescue, they take courage from the images they hear proclaimed.
God, they hear, is patient and is a God who saves. He has revealed
Himself as Savior in Jesus Christ, the righteous who dies for the unrighteous, now alive in the Spirit, reigning in heaven at God's right
hand, ruling angels, authorities, powers. As God sheltered Noah
through the flood of His just retribution, so God in Christ will preserve
them through the death that the sin of their kind makes inevitable, guiding them safely through it into life with Him forever. He will protect
them through physical death by delivering them from spiritual death;
for they are the unrighteous Christ died for, who must appeal to Him
for a clear conscience, so they can be cleansed from their sin and live
the new life that triumphs over death. The Faithful are those who have
already made this appeal by boarding the sturdy ark of Baptism and
becoming part of the perfect number of those chosen to be rescued.
For eight is the number of Resurrection, the number of perfection: while
God rested from Creation on the seventh day, it was on the eighth Christ
rose, leading in the New Creation of eternal life with Him. To say the
passengers on Baptism's ark are eight is to say they are those dead in
sin, resurrected by His rising, the perfect number God elects to save.

As the catechumens consider the nature of the means by which they
will be rescued from death, which the Faithful explain is Baptism, they
perceive the images the Faithful proclaim fitting together in yet another
pattern that illumines their salvation. They see that the waters of Bap-
Rom 6   tism are themselves the waters of death, for that self that would be God,
for that self that will not love. Those who drown their disobedience
in this font can rise up free from its eternal consequence. The catechumens need not fear this death; they have heard God promise not to
annihilate by water. It is only their death that will die there; who they
were born to be will come to life. For the wood of Christ's obedience
Exod 15:23-25 makes the bitter waters sweet, changes waters of death to those which
Ambrose, *De* bring true life. The catechumens understand that the Church is telling
Mysteriis 14 them that as they give themselves over to death in the waters of Baptism, they can be washed by the faithful death and resurrection of Jesus

Christ, and join the company of those who are borne safely by these waters to a new life. But the cleansing imparted by these waters is neither outward nor superficial. It brings a profound change in status toward God, His gift of an intimate relationship restored through their contact with the power of Christ's resurrection.

Whether the catechumens think of Baptism as the ship of their salvation, or as the mortal flood for their purification, as always they find themselves confronted with a choice between opposites: unrighteousness, and righteousness; death in the flesh, and life in the Spirit; disobedience leading to destruction, and obedience leading to salvation; the dirt of guilt, and a clear conscience. As they use these opposites to chart their course, the catechumens have a clearer sense of where they are. The Faithful have offered them rescue from the death of their disobedience, invited them to come aboard the ark of salvation and help make up the perfect number of the elect; soon they will give their answer. "Baptism, which corresponds to this, now saves you, not as a removal of dirt from the body but as an appeal to God for a clear conscience, through the resurrection of Jesus Christ, who has gone into heaven and is at the right hand of God, with angels, authorities, and powers subject to him."

By the light of the readings the catechumens have seen that their predicament is not hopeless, they need not drown in death. The first reading proclaimed that God is a rescuer, who seeks a relationship with them through which He will save them; the psalm sang of how God acts in that covenant, what it is like to live in relationship with Him. Now the epistle has explained the means by which they can enter this relationship in which they are rescued, yet they must still know one thing more: how do *they* act in this relationship, and how can they learn to live this way? For those who have taken refuge on this ship, embraced by the sturdy hold of Christ's faithfulness, are themselves known as Faithful. All who would navigate death's waters on this ark must pledge loyalty to its exalted Captain, be Faithful to the One who now rules even angels; His orders are: belay the swagger of their selfishness, and walk in servant-love. How can we learn to walk this way, the catechumens wonder. "Please sir," they ask the Captain, "How can we learn this stance of obedient self-giving, so we can keep our balance on your faithful ship, no matter what the raging of the waves?" "If you would serve me, follow me," He answers; "where I am, my servant will also be."

John 12:26

℣ Man does not live on bread alone,
but on every word that comes from the mouth of God.

Matt 4:4

The Spirit drove Jesus out into the wilderness. And he was in the wilderness forty days, tempted by Satan; and he was with the wild beasts; and the angels ministered to him.

Now after John was arrested, Jesus came into Galilee, preaching the gospel of God, and saying, "The time is fulfilled, and the kingdom of God is at hand; repent, and believe in the gospel."

Mark 1:12-15

"Follow me," He said, and now the catechumens find themselves driven with Him to the wilderness to spend forty days training in faithfulness as He once did. As they watch how He learned obedience and imitate it, they will learn how to be Faithful, how to give their lives before all else to loving service of God and all those He sends them to care for; they will learn to walk inspired not by the deadly No that ever directs their thoughts away from love, but by His life-giving Yes.

And as His Yes was strengthened by being tested by the Adversary, so will it be for them. It was that Adversary, after all, who first prompted their race in that desire to dominate, that No to Love that brought death's deep upon them. To escape this doom the catechumens must allow that No to be replaced by Christ's self-giving Yes. They must struggle with the one who ever murmurs in their mind "I will not serve," who continually stirs up that No in them, and learn to defeat him and his deadly whisper. His name *is* Destroyer; so that they will not escape the dark waters of death into which he lured their race, he will lie to them as he lied to their first parents. Building on their very fear of the death he led them to, he will seek to convince them that repeating the No will improve their life, whereas Yes to God will kill them. The Deceiver will focus his attack on the three areas in which they are most vulnerable to clinging to their selfish No by preferring something to God and life in the Spirit of His love: material possessions and security; human love and esteem; and power. The catechumens will find themselves engaged in a desperate contest, yet as they resist the Deceiver's assaults, they will find themselves growing stronger in that stance of faithful self-giving that they came to this strange proving ground to learn.

John Milton,
Paradise Lost
Rev 9:11

Deut 8:2ff.
Hos 2:14ff.

The place the Lord has brought the catechumens for this final time of training is the place where His people have ever learned obedience through testing, and have lived out their betrothal to the Faithful One whom the catechumens ask to make them Faithful: the wilderness. As the One they follow here faced the testing that confirmed His faithfulness in this desolate place, alone, so the catechumens' struggle against their selfish No will be fought in the wilderness of their hearts. Their ultimate reckoning before God will be alone; their consent to Christ's faithful Yes He will breathe into them at Baptism cannot be made by anyone but them.

Yet the catechumens are not completely alone these forty days, for if this bleak place of proving is barren of human habitations, it *is* frequented by wild beasts, fierce imaginings of what their Yes to God could mean which appear unbidden and untamed roam their minds at will. Their Adversary will continually focus the catechumens' attention on these ferocious prowlers, to terrify them into fleeing the contest and thus remaining subject to their mortal No. Always this Deceiver will manipulate their fear of death by seeking to convince them that ultimately what they need to sustain their existence is something other than God, that trusting God rather than this thing, loving God or fellow more than this thing, will lead to their extinction.

When the beastly spectre of material want appears, the Deceiver is ready to point out in detail all the horrifying features of its anatomy. "*So*, you want to give your life to Him, give Him all you have? *What if* He calls you to serve the poor full time and live in poverty yourself? How would you like to live in hunger, cold in winter, in constant worry over health care, even shelter? How would you like to go through life wearing what others had thrown out, clad in stains and holes and missing buttons, never even looking like who you are, but as who someone else no longer wants to be? How could you bear to live without vacations or a car? You can't give that Controller a blank check—you never know what He will take! Life is short and old age racked with illness and uncertainty. You must take care of yourself— no one else will. Acquire what you can and enjoy it; this is what gives you existence; this is how death is defied!"

If the catechumens stand fast, refusing to give ground to such feral forms in which their No presents itself to them, other savage shapes confront them—this time of life bereft of human love—and the Deceiver quickly calls attention to them. "*So*, you want to give your life to Him, love Him above all others? *What if* your family—parents, brothers, sisters, kin—disown you because you become His follower? What if His call to you deprives you of your right to married love and children? What if your loyal service in His cause is unappreciated— scorned? your friends reject you, you are abandoned to an early grave, alone? This love of God beyond all other loves goes much too far. Manipulate others to get the esteem you need, and enjoy their adulation; this is what gives you existence; this is how death is defied!"

And if the catechumens still hold their ground, they will find themselves beseiged by their protean No in yet a third onslaught of wild fears of what God theoretically might ask, this time fears of powerlessness; the Deceiver cheers on their brutal rampage through the catechumens' minds. "*So*, you want to give your life to Him, be ruled by His command? *What if* you make that unconditional surrender, and He leaves you unprotected, unable to defend yourself against whatever would destroy you? How can you yield your will to such a Master? His priorities are not the same as yours—see how He treated His own Son?! You must control or be controlled; the more you dominate, the less can harm you. This is what gives you existence; this is how death is defied!"

As the catechumens struggle to keep their balance in the stance of faithful self-giving through this stampede of threatening apparitions, they see more clearly what is at stake in this contest: What do they affirm as true giver of life, alone strong enough to deliver them from death? What alone is of such unsurpassable worth that they can—must—base their lives on it? Is it God, and therefore love of God and neighbor no matter what it costs, or is it something—anything—else? For the Spirit does not drive them to the wilderness to coerce them into masochistically depriving themselves of anything they truly need to live. Rather, as they grapple with the Adversary's lies of how giving their lives to God will destroy them, they discover what they are so terrified of losing that they fear to entrust it to the care of a God of infinite compassion. God is not necessarily asking those preparing for Baptism to take up some special manner of life that is not the common vocation of all Christians, but to be willing to offer their entire lives to His loving call to them, whatever it may be. The Lenten testing will reveal to those who would be Faithful what they in fact are faithful to, in what areas of their lives they must learn to stand more firmly in Christ's Yes, not leaning into No.

To learn this stance of obedient servant, the catechumens must take as model the One they followed to this wilderness, study how He triumphed in this contest, and imitate it. Each time they find themselves tempted to seek ultimate security in something other than God, they must reaffirm God as only true source of life, alone deserving to be loved over all; each time they find themselves slipping into the posture of self-gratification, they must stop clutching self-fulfillment and reach out in loving service. Yet in the catechumens' attempts to practice Christ's obedience, He does not leave them to the frailty of their own efforts, made futile by the weakness they were born with, but gives them His obedience; each time they falter, they must turn to Him for strength.

And as they do, the catechumens discover that wild beasts are not their only visitors in this wilderness testing, but there are angels, too. For though the Faithful cannot fight the catechumens' battles for them, nor break their bondage to their mortal No, they can minister as messengers of the truth that does set free. "See how these beastly thoughts as they go charging through your minds, raise so much dust it clouds your vision," these angels warn their charges. "It is through such confusion that the Deceiver works; he will make it seem that God is asking something which, if you grant it, will destroy you. This is the lie he has told our race from the beginning, to keep us from surrendering to the Love that will free us from his grasp and give us life. The truth is: if that is what you think you see, either God is not asking what you fear, or—if He is—it will bring life and not destruction in a way you can't yet see. We are baptized not into a life of teeth-gritting self-denial, but of letting His Spirit speak His Yes in us. Do not be discouraged to find you are unsteady in Christ's stance of faithful love; He will not

1 Cor 10:13   let you be tried beyond your strength. The contest is only to show you where you need His help; discover your weakness and learn to receive His strength."

The catechumens remember what brought them to this strange wilderness: they asked to learn how to be loyal subjects to the King who is Ruler of the angels and of the saving ship on which they seek

"At the
Name of
Jesus,"
C.M. Noel

to serve. They see that each time they repeat His Yes, they draw nearer to His reigning over them; as they crown Him as their Captain in temptation's hour, they will learn the obedience to serve under His command. As they fix their eyes more closely on the One they followed here, they see Him turn and speak directly to them: "The time is fulfilled and the kingdom of God is at hand; repent and believe in the Gospel."

[Relationship
of readings
to each
other]

As the reader closes the Lectionary, the catechumens find the images revealed by the brilliance of the Word still vivid in their minds. Through these images the Faithful have shown them that while all who rebel against Love must be swallowed by death's waves, it is the way of their God to rescue those who would obey from their inborn tendency to self-destruction. He has offered them a covenant, a faithful relationship that will give them life, sealed in the faithfulness of His own Son. Those who have accepted this covenant have pointed out to the catechumens how on the Cross, as through a prism, the pure light of Christ's obedience refracts into the full spectrum of God's mercy, embracing all the globe with faithful love. To accept this pledge, to be rescued by this mercy, the catechumens need only board Baptism's ark, yet they need sea legs to be faithful mariners. So the Faithful led them to the Lord who now invites them to feel the Spirit at their backs, driving them with Him to the wilderness, where they can learn His faithfulness. And now they must decide if they will follow, for the One who

2 Cor 6:2   proclaims good news says now is the time to repent, now is the time

to believe, now is His kingdom open to them if they come forward and ask.

The catechumens think of the waters of destruction, how they are death for all who disobey Love, but carry the obedient on the ark to life in a new covenant. They will accept this covenant, put death to death, the catechumens decide; Noah's heirs come to escort them to enlist for service on the saving ship. But first the seasoned sailors must make sure the new recruits are stout enough to make it through the wilderness training now ahead for all. Have they listened to the Word these many months as it was proclaimed to them? Have they walked by it and thus stayed on faith's journey's path? Have they sought the companionship of their guides on the way, have they prayed with them in the assembly which constitutes them as who they are?

The sponsors have given their consent; now the catechumens are asked for theirs. Do you wish to stop choking on the dark waters of your No, and be resussitated by His Breath of Yes? Do you wish to be betrothed to that great Love, who enclasps you with the rainbow as a ring? Do you wish to book your passage on this ark, join ship's company and learn ship's faithful ways? "Since you have already heard the call of Christ, you must now express your response to that call clearly and in the presence of the whole Church. Therefore, do you wish to enter fully into the life of the Church through the sacraments of Baptism, Confirmation, and the Eucharist?" The catechumens think again how all must face death; there is no avoiding its black waters. But the ark of Christ's love is strong as death, the dark floods of death can't drown it. "We do," they say.

The names of the Elect are proclaimed and, as always, the Faithful provision them by their prayer, this time requesting for them the special equipment they will need for the Lenten trial ahead. "My dear Elect, you have set out with us on the road that leads to the glory of Easter. Christ will be your way, your truth, and your life. Until we meet again for the scrutinies, walk always in his peace."

As they gird themselves for the final stages of their journey, the newly Elect know they are not alone. Those once dead, who will never die again, will ever point them to the path of life. The Elect depart. Having begun this day overwhelmed by death's black sin-filled waters, in forty days they will board the ship whose hull is hewn of death for death and sealed with Resurrection.

Margin notes:
RCIA 131B

RCIA 132

Songs 8:6-7

RCIA 134, 135
RCIA 136

(see above,
pp. 26–27)

. . . God's Word to the Faithful is also His Word to them. . .

(Year C)   Or is it? Even as they present themselves for election, the catechumens catch the dull echoes of this leaden question sounding in the corners of their minds. Does this Word *really* have something to say to them? Before they set out on faith's journey, the catechumens had ignored such questions, allowing them to be drowned out by a din of distractions, but now the catechumenate's times of silent listening in prayer have honed their spiritual hearing, made their spiritual perception more acute. Now they can pick up promptings of God's Spirit they would previously have been deaf to, but they can also hear more clearly the suggestions of the Deceiver. "The-one-who-makes-the-world-to-wander," the ancients called this Liar, who leads the world astray into destruction. To each person born he speaks the lies most likely to deceive him into unintentionally straying into his domain, coming under his deadly power. To the catechumens, as to so many in their age, he has addressed himself as Spectre of Meaninglessness, Spirit of Alienation.

*Apostolic
Constitutions
VII, 32*

Does this Word say anything at all to *me?* The reverberations of the Deceiver's question can be heard clearly in the catechumens' minds: "It is all right for these Faithful; they grew up with all these stories of a loving God, for them, it's a natural expression of their culture. But for *me,* it is different. What reason is there for me to think there is any meaning to life, anything that will ultimately make sense of things, when all I see around me is absurdity? And if there is finally no meaning to anything in life, then what meaning is there even to *me?* What gives me identity—what do I belong to and who am I? I must be adult and free myself from childish wishful thinking: there is no meaning; I am part of nothing, going nowhere, I am nobody."

But if the catechumens find their minds growing heavy, lulled by the unceasing beat of this hypnotic threnody, they can still pick out the counterpoint of God's Spirit: "Free themselves"—is true freedom what they seek? Does accepting the ascendancy of Meaninglessness bring them freedom, or does it ensnare them in the cruelest slavery? What of those they know who are enthralled by the false sophistication of the Deceiver's mesmerizing dirge, who live their lives with Meaninglessness as master—in what kind of freedom do these people live? Meaninglessness drives them to rise early, labor brutally and long, to prevent being paralyzed by the agony of despair; yet since all they do is undertaken to distract from Meaninglessness, it is itself thus meaningless: their toil is futile, they will have no fruit of their labor. And Meaninglessness keeps them from getting close to any with whom they might be tempted to seek meaning; those governed by No Meaning have no place where they belong: they are never at home but ever aliens, wondering who they are. Such is the "freedom" of those who bow to the Spirit of this Age; Meaninglessness lays on them hard bondage, they are crushed under its weight, their agonized struggle brings them only death. Look for yourself and see—is this the freedom that you seek? God's Spirit asks.

As the catechumens listen to the steady point and counterpoint of this argument in their minds, they realize that they, too, are still children of their age, haunted by the Spectre of Meaninglessness, afflicted by Alienation. They begin to perceive that they are not free as they had thought, but are oppressed in many ways, and cannot free themselves by their own strength. This is why they have come today, they remind themselves, to hear again that Word which alone has the power to deliver them, and draw them further on their journey from unbelief to faith. "Tell us again," they entreat the Faithful simply by their presence, "tell us yet once more why you think that there is Meaning, and what that Meaning is, and who you are to dare make such a claim."

The Faithful respond, as always, by telling the story entrusted to them, the story that has become their story, too, and is the only explanation of their lives:

> Moses said to the people, "The priest shall take the basket [of first fruits] from your hand, and set it down before the altar of the LORD your God.
> "And you shall make response before the LORD your God, 'A wandering Aramean was my father; and he went down into Egypt and sojourned there, few in number; and there he became a nation, great, mighty, and populous. And the Egyptians treated us harshly, and afflicted us, and laid upon us hard bondage. Then we cried to the LORD the God of our fathers, and the LORD heard our voice, and saw our affliction, our toil, and our oppression; and the LORD brought us out of Egypt with a mighty hand and an outstretched arm, with great terror, with signs and wonders; and he brought us into this place and gave us this land, a land flowing with milk and honey. And behold, now I bring the first fruit of the ground, which thou, O LORD, hast given me.' And you shall set it down before the LORD your God, and worship before the LORD your God."

"One whom we have come from was a wanderer, and our people have been slaves," the Faithful say. "We, too, know what it means to be oppressed. But what our forebears handed on to us, this we proclaim to you: when from sweat and groans of harshest bondage they cried out, there was a Mighty One who heard and had compassion. He revealed Himself as Freer of the Captives; with power He brought our

1 Cor 2:12

Deut 26:4-10

parents out and gave them their own land, exchanged the bitterness of their bondage for freedom's flowing honey. Where in slavery the only fruit of their forced labor was death, the place He gave them provided them with life-giving fruit, which they could offer back to Him with joy. This is the Meaning those who experienced it have handed on to us, and we have seen that it is true in our own lives. Meaning is that Love that saved our forebears from Egypt, and delivers us from all oppressing us today. For we too have been enslaved, though not in Egypt, bound like you, by the Spirit of this Age; yet when we cried out to the One who freed our parents, He showed that He is Savior still today. He brought us to a place where we could dwell in freedom, and know who we are and why we are alive. To worship Him who gives all things their meaning, this is what gives meaning to our lives. He has brought us together and given us identity: we are His worshippers who offer Him the first fruits of all He gives, for we know everything we have is gift from Him. Believe the story we speak, and you, too, can be free!"

The Faithful know the syllables of their story are not magic in themselves, automatically releasing those captivated by the steady, seductive rhythm of the Deceiver's lies. Yet as the words are proclaimed, their proclamation functions as a graceful flute, to concentrate the Spirit's breath for human hearing. Through that flute the Spirit breathes the Word in power, the one melody so true it silences all else; the Faithful know its golden purity can arouse in the catechumens the faith through which they will receive the salvation from Meaninglessness they long for.

As the catechumens listen to the words and begin to hear the Word, they become aware that its melody contains phrases musically depicting God, the Faithful, and themselves. In the phrases which are word-paintings of them, the catechumens hear themselves depicted as slaves who need to be set free. Not only are they bound by sin and their own inevitable death, but their minds are dominated by the Spirit of this Age, the *Zeitgeist* of Meaninglessness and Alienation. They exhaust their time desperately striving to accomplish things so that they will not have to face the futility of their existence, and other people become simply means through which they try to achieve this self-deception. But if the catechumens will cry out from this captivity of their minds, they will find that there is meaning: there is One who hears the cry of the afflicted and *cares*, and reaches out a mighty hand to save. God is the One who rescues the helpless from oppression, with terrifying wonders and signs of love. Through mighty waters He will lead the catechumens into a new life in His own Spirit—and where the Spirit of the Lord is, there is freedom; and this Spirit will also give them identity,

2 Cor 3:17

making them His adopted children. In these waters He will drown the Meaninglessness and Alienation which oppress the catechumens, and they will know the glorious liberty of the children of God. This life of freedom, this life in the Spirit into which He brings them is lived out in the Church, abounding with all graces; here He feeds His children on the pure spiritual milk of the Word with the sweet richness of sacramental rite. Their lives will be fruitless no longer, but bear the fruit of the Spirit; they will find meaning in coming before Him with His people and making grateful return of all He gives to them.

Rom 8;21

Gal 5:22

The phrases describing the Faithful portray them as those God has delivered from wandering and oppression, affliction and trial, whose identity is constituted in worshipping Him, standing before Him and serving Him, offering to Him before all else. They are heirs of Israel, children of the wandering Aramean, those who bring first fruits and tell the story of why.

Eucharistic
Prayer II

The melody of the Word has begun and ended with the opposites between which the catechumens find themselves: bondage, and their own land; affliction, and milk and honey; oppression, and freedom. The catechumens realize that through its phrases, the Faithful have given answer to their questions:

" 'Why do we think there is meaning?'—those who were captives told us of the One who made them free, who is Meaning and gives meaning to all things."

" 'What is this Meaning?'—that there is a Love, all-powerful, who reaches out and helps—*that* is the meaning of all things," the Faithful say. "The meaning of life is to know Him, to know Him is to worship Him, all who worship Him belong to Him, they always know who they are. The meaning of existence, the reason we were created, is to worship this Love who hears and saves, and return to Him love's due."

" 'Who are we to say this?'—we are the children of those slaves, who were ourselves set free, delivered from a different kind of bondage: we used to have no meaning, we used to be nobody, once we were no people, but now we are God's People. He gives us identity, makes us who we are, as we come to adore and return the love He gives."

Hos 2:28,
Rom 9:25-26
1 Pet 2:10

The Faithful have given their answer. They know *they* cannot make the catechumens Faithful, give them the faith to believe in what they've said, but to be Faithful to the God who works such wonders in their midst is to ever tell the story of His deeds.

"And you shall set it down before the Lord your God, and worship before the Lord your God." The catechumens find their hearts resonating with the strong melody of the Word; long enough have they been burdened with the angst of the Spirit of their Age, long enough have they been slaves. They want to escape the dominion of the Spectre of

Meaninglessness, Spirit of Alienation, who prevents them from finding the place of worship in freedom, and thus knowing Meaning as the Faithful do. "Tell us more of this One who gives your lives their meaning; and show us how to cry out for His help."

Ps 91:15b   R/ Be with me, Lord, when I am in trouble.

He who dwells in the shelter of the Most High,
    who abides in the shadow of the Almighty,
will say to the Lord, "My refuge and my fortress;
    my God in whom I trust."
No evil shall befall you,
    no scourge come near your tent.
For he will give his angels charge of you
    to guard you in all your ways.
Because he cleaves to me in love, I will deliver him;
    I will protect him, because he knows my name.
When he calls to me, I will answer him;
    I will be with him in trouble,
Ps 91:1-2,   I will rescue him and honor him.
10-11, 14-15

With those before them delivered from bondage in Egypt, with the Faithful and all who have been freed from captivity to anything that hindered them from worshipping and serving the only One who can—and must—be worshipped, the catechumens join in crying out for aid. The Faithful lead them in this song, not only to answer their request, and teach the catechumens how to make contact with the awesome Freer of the Captives, but also to continue their story of God's care by deepening their description of who He is and what it means to be part of His People. He is almighty, they sing, Most High over all things, yet He can be trusted. He is a fortress for those who take refuge in Him, and protects them from any evil that might destroy them; He answers those who love Him when they call, is with them in distress, delivers them and gives them glory. The Faithful sing of themselves as those who dwell in the shelter, the shadow, of God, those who trust Him; they cling to Him in love and are guarded by angels, protected because they know Phil 2:9-11 His name—know who it is who is truly Lord of all, before whom alone every knee shall bow. The catechumens hear themselves depicted as those who are in trouble, but if they will make the shelter of this all-powerful One their abode, He will be present with them in their trouble; He will answer their call and rescue them.

It is fitting for the Faithful to invite the catechumens to join in this song today, for today the catechumens have arrived at a crucial juncture on their journey. In order to go on, they must recognize and ad-

Eph 2:2ff.

mit publicly that they are indeed in bondage to the Spirit of their Age, and ask the only One who has the power to free them for salvation. As the catechumens cry for help, the Faithful encourage them, urging them to join them in cleaving to the Lord in love so they can be delivered, telling them that as long as they live under His protection, no Spectre of Meaninglessness nor any scourge of Satan can harm them. Today they would pledge themselves to living their lives in the shelter of the Most High. Through the psalm the Faithful reassure the catechumens with a comforting picture of what that life is like, and the reminder that the Lord, too, is pledging Himself to them, to rescue and honor them.

"Be with me, Lord, when I am in trouble." The catechumens find that as they join the singing, the purity of the melody of the Word transports them into the place of worship they sought. They are being assimilated into a community that is most itself when standing before their God and worshipping, by themselves worshipping; while the Faithful have taught the catechumens from the beginning the praise that is the dominant theme of that worship, they also teach them the important variations, such as trustfully seeking help in trouble. In the very act of repeating the refrain with the Faithful, the catechumens are already growing in trust and coming more fully under the protection of the One who guards the Faithful.

And yet, the catechumens reflect, the Faithful say they are protected because they know His name: "We, too, want to be delivered from the Deceiver's dominion; we, too, want to be protected from his lies. Where

Eph 4:8

can we learn His Name—this Freer of the Captives? Must we go far above the heavens to the throne of this 'Most High'?—For this Word

Rom 10:6-7

that saves us, must we search the depths?"

> What does the scripture say? The word is near you, on your lips and in your heart (that is, the word of faith which we preach); because, if you confess with your lips that Jesus is Lord and believe in your heart that God raised him from the dead, you will be saved. For man believes with his heart and so is justified, and he confesses with his lips and so is saved. The scripture says "No one who believes in him will be put to shame." For there is no distinction between Jew and Greek; the same Lord is Lord of all and bestows his riches upon all who call upon him.

Rom 10:8-13

> For, "every one who calls upon the name of the Lord will be saved."

As the Faithful give their answer, the melody of the Word flows on without seeming to have changed, yet somehow its resonance is richer and fuller, and, though the catechumens would not have thought it possible, even more glorious than before: "Once He sang Himself in our own flesh; today He sings Himself in this our song. The Word you seek, the Name you seek, is near us; He is 'Boundless-Love-That-Saves-and-Would-Save-You.' "

The catechumens have asked the Faithful whether they must go to distant realms to learn the name of the Almighty One who can set them free and protect them, so they can ask for His help; through the epistle the Faithful respond that this saving Word is near them even as the Scripture is proclaimed, and that His Name is Jesus. Yet the Faithful know that for the catechumens to understand this answer to their question, so that they can actually receive the freedom from oppression they seek, they must know more. To be free from their Oppressor, the catechumens need to understand how he exercises his control over them: by what means did he capture them, and what are those bonds by which he keeps them so weighed down they can't escape?

"The first of our race were free," the Faithful explain, "until they listened to the guile of the Deceiver. He urged them to ignore the Loving Truth that orders all things, to seek a more self-satisfying knowledge; by heeding his lies and rejecting that Love, they left the service of the Truth and came into the dominion of that Liar. When they found he sore oppressed them and sought to flee, they discovered that because they freely accepted his lies, they willingly made themselves his bondservants, so they and their children would ever be his slaves. This refusal to believe the Loving Truth and thus be ruled by it, this sin, was the first bond by which he held our race, and led us into even heavier bondage. For by this bond of our rejection of the Truth, he drew us into all the false actions that result from unbelief; each action is another selfish sin which adds more weight to our bonds. To be free of this bondage, we needed to be freed not only from the Deceiver, but from the self-forged bonds of sin that hold us fast. Only Truth Himself, who had never bowed to the lies of the Deceiver, had the power to release us from his grasp and destroy his hold on us; only Love unfettered by the weight of selfish sin could break the bonds that held us. So the Truth who from afar once showed himself as Freer of the Captives, now came in blood and flesh to smash the Liar; with the mighty hand of obedient love He snapped the bonds of sin, with the terror of His outstretched arm, He led our race to freedom. To all who call on this Jesus, acknowledging their need to be set free from their self-forged weight of sin and His power to release them, He will replace those bonds with the freedom of His righteousness. But if you want to experience the full salvation He would give you, you must see how the lies of the Deceiver keep you from knowing that Truth that makes us free, and by what bonds of sin these lies keep you enslaved."

The catechumens realize that they have been collaborators with their Oppressor, and that they must identify and renounce their own share in their oppression to be truly free of it. They see how the Deceiver has lied to their race from the beginning, and how, because their parents assented to his falsehood, they themselves were so inclined when he addressed them in the guise of the Spectre of Meaninglessness, Spirit of Alienation—an approach that sways the allegiance of many in their age. They must discover how this willingly entertaining the suggestions of the Spectre of Meaninglessness has led to futility in their thinking, darkness in their minds, and what sins their wandering from the Truth has led them into. To say there is no Meaning is to say there is no God, and to end up as their own gods by default; once the Spectre has led them into the shackles of the sin of unbelief, they find themselves bound with idolatry and selfishness as well. And if they are gods, then all others are reduced to lesser beings, existing only to serve them as slavish devotees; thus alienated from the rest of humankind, they are weighed down with anger, resentment, and jealousy when their primacy goes unacknowledged. Yet the One who came to preach liberty to captives will show them how the Deceiver holds them bound, and will help them lift up their bonds to Him to be destroyed.

Eph 4:17-18

Luke 4:18

As the catechumens listen to the melody of the Word, they find they can again distinguish tonal images of God, the Faithful, and themselves. God, they hear, is Lord of all creation and all people. He is Savior to all who call upon His name, and raised Jesus from the dead to bring salvation. They hear the Faithful portrayed as those who did call on this Lord, believe in Him, confess Him, and were saved; the One who made them Faithful will not let them be put to shame. Now they preach this liberating word of faith to the catechumens, showing them how the Deceiver has lured them into sin, so that they are enslaved by it, and must admit they are sinners who need a Savior to make them righteous. If they do and confess the One the Father raised up to save them, they will be released from the bondage of sin and the Deceiver who uses it to oppress them, and receive the freedom of salvation they long for—they will be free indeed. The salvation He offers them is the same gift He has given to those born into the family of the Faithful, for He bestows on them, as on all who call upon Him, riches without distinction.

John 8:36

The catechumens consider what they have heard this day. The Faithful have told them frankly that they are slaves, oppressed by the Deceiver, who manipulates them through their rejection of the Truth into dragging the weight of every kind of sin. Yet, if they cry for His help, there is One whose love will rescue them and give them refuge. Jesus is the name the Freer of the Captives gives His Love; His name alone can fell their ancient foe. As the decision not to believe in the Loving Truth that orders all things put the catechumens in bondage to sin, so

"A Mighty Fortress," Martin Luther

their decision of faith God works in them will lead to their justification and release from sin's bonds; for, as they inwardly believe in Jesus as the One the Father gave victory over sin and the death it brings, and proclaim it aloud, the catechumens, too, will experience salvation.

"For 'everyone who calls upon the name of the Lord will be saved.'" The catechumens think they understand: all they must do is commit themselves this day to coming under the protection of Jesus, and they will be freed once and for all from their oppression by the Deceiver and their inclination to let his lies direct their actions. No more will they catch the hollow echoes of his accusing question in their thoughts, for their minds will be completely filled with the rich melody of the Word, and they will naturally walk to its rhythm, without even consciously trying. But the Faithful know that if the catechumens merely admire the beauty of the Word, and acknowledge its truth, they will soon stumble back into many of the bonds that they were freed from. For God does not so flood their minds with His Word that they are controlled by it like mindless robots. If they would be truly free from the patterns of sin in which the Deceiver has held them, and truly live

2 Cor 5:17   as a new creation, they must continually choose with His help to think and walk according to His Word. They must learn to be not only appreciative listeners to the Word's melody, but they must, empowered by His Spirit, willingly internalize it: learn it by heart so they can sing it with Him in their minds and gracefully walk to it. And their attempt to do this, and to walk free from the bonds by which the Deceiver holds them, will bring them into direct confrontation with him; it cannot be avoided: they must recognize his lies for what they are, and renounce them for the truth of the Word. "Come," the Faithful say, "there is yet more to understand. You must learn how to stay free from your Oppressor; you must learn how to defeat him when he attacks you and tries to lead you back into bondage. But the One who broke his power shows you how, and gives you the strength you need to fight."

Matt 4:4   ℣ Man does not live on bread alone,
but on every word that comes from the mouth of God.

Jesus, full of the Holy Spirit, returned from the Jordan, and was led by the Spirit for forty days in the wilderness, tempted by the devil. And he ate nothing in those days; and when they were ended, he was hungry. The devil said to him, "If you are the Son of God, command this stone to become bread."

And Jesus answered him, "It is written, 'Man shall not live by bread alone.'"

And the devil took him up, and showed him all the kingdoms of the world in a moment of time, and said to him, "To you I will give all this

authority and their glory; for it has been delivered to me, and I give it
to whom I will. If you, then, will worship me, it shall all be yours."

And Jesus answered him, "It is written, 'You shall worship the Lord
your God, and him only shall you serve.'"

And he took him to Jerusalem, and set him on the pinnacle of the
temple, and said to him, "If you are the Son of God, throw yourself down
from here; for it is written, 'He will give his angels charge of you, to
guard you,' and 'On their hands they will bear you up, lest you strike
your foot against a stone.'"

And Jesus answered him, "It is said, 'You shall not tempt the Lord
your God.'"

And when the devil had ended every temptation, he departed from
Luke 4:1-13   him until an opportune time.

If the power of the Spirit-charged Word the catechumens heard in
the psalm transported them into worship, now they find it has brought
them into battle. Their Adversary has not resigned himself to losing
them, but adopted a new strategy. What if the catechumens would
profess Jesus as Lord and source of all meaning in their lives? As long
as they don't actually live as if this were true, they are not completely
lost to him; they might even be useful to him as advertisements for
his claim that Christianity is sheer hypocrisy. The Deceiver must make
sure that whatever the catechumens *say* they believe, they still take
for granted the premises he has established in their minds in his guise
as Spectre of Meaninglessness, Spirit of Alienation. As long as they
(without being aware of it) live out their lives as if there were no ultimate Meaning, they will seek to create their own meaning to avoid
despair, and rely on things other than God to deliver them from
Meaninglessness; in particular, they will dedicate themselves to the ac-
quisition of material possessions, power, and human esteem, and allow their daily lives to be dictated by efforts to acquire them. As long
Rom 12:2   as their minds are still conformed to the Spirit of their Age, they will
put their devotion to these three things ahead of their service to God,
and they will not be free of their Oppressor and the bonds of sin which
his lies lead them into.

. . . The catechumens have already heard so much today, that as
the Gospel begins it seems as if their minds are beginning to wander,
or at least picking up an all-too-familiar echo: "How hungry I am; all
this penitential fasting just makes me think more about food. And food
isn't the only thing I need; there are so many things I want. But if I
am child of God, if God really loves me, I can invest my time figuring
out how I can get as much of everything as I want, then just 'go for
it' and revel in it. I deserve it, as the commercials say; if anyone really
deserves the best of everything, it's me. And if there's anything left over,

I can save it, or maybe give a little to the 'less fortunate'; but everyone knows when people are 'less fortunate' it's their own fault, and if you give them much at all you just encourage them to be lazy. No, the good things in life, as many as I can get hold of, are given to me to enjoy for my own sake—they give meaning to my life. The Faithful say God

1 Pet 4:10

gives us everything we have as gift so we can be His stewards who seek His will for how we should offer it back to Him or others, and what He would have us keep for our own use. But this can lead to unhealthy self-deprivation. If I am child of God, if God really loves me, I should have whatever I want whenever I want it. Be a discerning steward? No, no reason. No."

"Yes." And now the catechumens hear the Word's melody taken up by a Voice. "Yes, be a steward, and don't listen to such lies: remem-

Luke 12:19, 16:13

ber, 'eat, drink, and be merry' was the slogan of a fool, and do not think that you can serve two masters. Love urges you, don't labor for

John 6:27

this bread that sustains you only for a moment, but for the Word of life that keeps you alive forever; say Yes to His Word of love and let it feed you. Let Him show you how to share the goods He gives: it is in His Word that you will find true meaning. Yes, be a steward. See, I fought for this Yes and give it to you, if you would learn to speak it. Yes to His Word, His will, as what nourishes you with meaning, and not your selfish grabbing. Yes."

As the catechumens seek to synchronize their thinking with the true rhythm of the Voice, they are again distracted by the Deceiver's persistent dissonance. "When I look around and see what's really out there, I want another job—one where I can have more control, with more people under me, and no one who can boss me. You know, the more you take control in life, the better off you are, protected from all those waiting to control you—use you for their advantage against your own. The best job I can get, that's what I need, where I can use my authority to fortify my own interests. The Faithful say God allows people to have positions of power so we can use power to serve others, seek justice and protection for all; they say we shouldn't compulsively claw our way to the highest place, but ask Him where He's gifted us to be of greatest help. But anyone can see that this is self-destructive. If you live in this world you must live by its rules, and they are clear: be master of all you can so you can enjoy the security that makes life meaningful. Be a devoted servant? No, no point. No."

"Yes." Again the Voice. "Yes, be a servant, and don't fall for such deception. See how our common Enemy once tried to sell me the glory that was my inheritance by right, at the cost of betraying my own Father! Now he seeks to swindle you in the same way. For to 'live by

John 12:31

the rules of this world' is to bow to the Ruler of this World, and make

Jas 4:4 | yourself an enemy of God; this is the price of pursuing power above all else. What would it profit you to gain any kingdom he could give,

Matt 16:26
Luke 12:32 | when in return you pay him with your soul? You do not need to seize the power of earthly kingdoms for protection: your Father has given a kingdom to you where all is yours and you are mine; this is all the

Luke 12:31 | security you need. Love exhorts you, seek first His kingship over you and worship Him; say Yes to His kingdom of love and be His servant, not your own master. He will show you how to use the power He gives you to bring help, not domination; and in loving service, not power, you'll find true meaning. Yes, be a servant. Hear, I fought for this Yes and give it to you, if you would learn to speak it. Yes to His kingship as what empowers you with meaning, and gives the only security that lasts forever. Yes."

As the catechumens seek to attune their thoughts to the true pitch of the Voice, the Deceiver's dull cacophony echoes on. "You know, it's really time I started getting more attention. I'm so much better than most people, I would be an inspiration; I should promote myself, let everyone see how wonderful I am. I should take every risk and set my-

Luke 4:9-11 | self up as high as I can; and since I'm God's child He'll catch me if I slip—it says so in the Bible. I need approval no matter what I have to do to get applause; without the praise of others, what meaning is there to life? The Faithful say we shouldn't base our lives on striving after human approbation, nor tell God how to affirm us on our terms; they say God made us not to grasp at adulation to gratify ourselves,

Eph 4:2 | but to trust His love for us and share it freely—defer to each other out of love for Christ. But this just leads to masochistic self-abasement. If I am child of God, if God really loves me, He'll increase my self-esteem by making others adore me. Be a humble lover? No, no way! No."

"Yes. Yes, be a lover and don't be flattered by deceit; a haughty

Prov 16:18 | spirit only courts destruction. Don't try to make the Father prove what He's already given, as if the price He paid to free you had no worth. Love pleads with you, don't strive to build up your self-worth with

1 Pet 5:6 | the fickle praise of others, but humble yourself to accept the faithful

John 15:13 | love of God. Say Yes to the worth I gave you in laying down my life; no greater value can anyone give to you. Let me show you how I have

Isa 49:16 | graven you on the palms of my hands, that you may know you are

Isa 43:4 | infinitely precious in my sight. Don't nullify the grace of God: if you

Gal 2:21 | accept as measure of your worth the esteem you extort from others, then I died to no purpose. Live by the mercy you cannot earn, and

John 13:34 | let it flow through you to others; in loving them as I have loved you,

Phil 2:3 | you will find the meaning of human relationships. It is the lowly who share my mind, counting others' needs more pressing than their own,

Luke 14:11 who can be raised up and exalted by my Father. Yes, be a lover. Believe, I fought for this Yes and give it to you, if you would learn to speak it. Yes to my love, my life, as what justifies your existence, and gives it its worth and meaning. Yes."

The catechumens try to bring their minds into harmony with the full richness of the Word, but the echoes of the Deceiver's single discordant note continue to bombard them with the monotony of a metronome: "No. No Meaning. No. No reason to be a steward. No. No God. No. No point in serving others. No. No Loving Truth. No. No way humble love is worth it. No. No Meaning. No." Yet as this confrontation with the Deceiver continually unfolds in the arena of their minds, the One who frees from all oppression will show them the Deceiver's strategy and the method by which He defeated him, so that once they are freed they do not step back into the shackles by which their Oppressor has held them.

He will show the catechumens how the Deceiver tried to tempt Him into being a different kind of Son of God, a different kind of Chosen Rescuer than the one God willed, to provide instant gratification to human needs in accord with self-centered human desires, rather than the Father's all-loving providence. The Deceiver employs a similar strategy with the catechumens, tempting them to think that they can live out their adoption as the Father's children on their own terms, that they can determine what use of possessions, power, and human relationships are right and good for them according to their own selfishly perceived "needs," rather than letting their use of them be determined by God's will, revealed in His Word. What Jesus would teach them through the account of His temptation is not that goods or power or esteem are bad in themselves, but that they are, as all creation, gifts of God which are given to be used according to His purpose so they can bring blessing; after all, the same Word that recounts Jesus' refusal to use divine power to create bread from a stone to satisfy the demands Matt 14:19ff. of Satan, also records that He multiplied the loaves to feed the hungry.

But Jesus would also make clear to them through His example that to pursue possessions or power or esteem for their own sake is to remain ensnared in the Deceiver's deadly lie that there is really no meaning beyond the things of this life—no ultimate Meaning, thus no Loving Truth ordering all things, no God. Bound by this lie, those who live as if there were no Meaning will inevitably be pulled back into all the false actions constituting the bondage of sin; they cannot walk in the freedom of the Loving Truth which alone gives life. What is at stake for the catechumens in their Lenten time of trial, then, is what will truly be the source of meaning in their lives, who will determine for them what their true needs are, what it means for them to be children of

God. Will it be the Loving Truth—God's saving love poured out in Jesus Christ—and the way He would order their lives as revealed in His Word? Or will it be the Spirit of their Age, whose strategy is to deceive them into being their own "gods," creating their own false "truth" and "meaning"?

During their forty days of testing the catechumens must come to recognize their Adversary's lies concerning what it means to live as God's child for the deadly deceptions they are, and the ways in which they allow those lies to determine their behavior; they must discover how, in spite of their intention to give their lives to God as followers of Christ, they are still influenced by the Spirit of their Age, and they must learn how to resist him so he will flee from them. They must be tested in every crucial way, for their Adversary will return: in Baptism Christians are born not into a life of effortless sanctity, but into battle with one who seeks every opportunity to rob them of their new freedom in the Spirit. To prepare for a lifetime of such testing, the catechumens must come to grips even now with the reality of temptation and their own weakness; they must become aware of how their own tendency to sin functions as a fifth column collaborating with their Adversary, and how he is ever ready to exploit that. Since the principal arena for this battle is their minds, the catechumens must learn to wear the helmet of salvation, learn to protect their thoughts with the truth of God's saving love in Christ.

Eph 6:17

This does not mean that when their Adversary seeks to penetrate their thoughts with the No to God that would keep them in bondage, they are solely dependent on the strength of their own mind and will to resist the force of his lies. The One who preceded them in this testing does not only reveal to them the strategy of the Deceiver, and teach them the Yes to the Loving Truth by which He defeated him; He actually gives them His own Yes as obedient Son of God by which He saved them from the Adversary's grasp—which He began to utter even in this wilderness—if only they are willing to speak it with Him. For as the Spirit led Jesus to His wilderness trial to manifest His Sonship through His Yes, so the Spirit who will make the catechumens sons leads them to this testing so they can learn this Yes—learn on an even deeper level to think and act as God's children.

Rom 8:14ff.

And as the catechumens learn to speak this Yes, to allow God's saving love to be the determinative Meaning of their lives, to enjoy goods, power, and relationships as God's gifts bestowed for His purposes, they will in fact begin to experience the new identity as children of God which acceptance of the Father's love as ultimate Meaning brings. They will also find that their acceptance of His love as Meaning gives meaning to human relationships. For as the catechumens become aware of the

Deceiver's influence over them and seek to be free of it, they will discover how the Spectre of Meaninglessness which encourages those of
their Age to be their own meaning, their own gods, has not only separated them from God, but also from others. As they learn to root their
lives, including all their relationships, in God's Word, the catechumens
will find that their obedience to the Truth purifies them so that they
know a sincere and heartfelt love for others; freed from selfishness,
they can be open to others for who they are and not what they can
be used for, and begin to be released from the isolation and alienation
of those ruled by Meaninglessness. They will discover that to be child
of God gives them not only a Father to whom they belong, but also
a home filled with brothers and sisters who are also His children.

    "And when the devil had ended every temptation, he departed from
Him until an opportune time." As the echoes of the Deceiver's mock-
ing question, "Is this really God's Word—for you?" temporarily sub-
side, the catechumens can turn all of their attention to recalling the main
themes of the Word's melody with which the Faithful have continued
to tell their story. The Faithful have told of how they cried out from
bondage and God delivered them from it and formed them into a
People, and how that same God would now free the catechumens from
the oppression of alienation and meaninglessness and make them, too,
part of His People. Those already freed have invited the catechumens
to join them as part of this rescued, worshipping, offering People, to
enter the life of freedom where, since God gives all that is life-giving,
all first fruits are given to Him; as they joined with the Faithful in the
psalm, the catechumens became part of the story of those who cried
for help and were saved. They heard that the Word that liberates is
near them, that they can begin to enter into salvation even now—not
by reciting a formula, but by the profound change in values and existential orientation that comes from entering a life of worshipping and
offering to God as part of His People. The Faithful have encouraged
the catechumens to learn to trust God and find meaning in His will
in three crucial areas where they are tempted to set themselves up as
their own arbiters of meaning, and have warned them that their rescue
is not without temptation and cannot be cause for presumption; as they
progress through Lent the catechumens will learn what Jesus learns in
the Gospel: what are, and what are not, the prerogatives of sonship.
The catechumens cannot help but notice how the verses promising God's
protection to His own they heard proclaimed in the psalm were quoted
by their Adversary when he tempted Christ. By showing them how
the very words that were so comforting in the psalm were used by the
Deceiver in his attempt to mislead Christ, the Faithful are telling the

1 Pet 1:22

[Relationship
of readings
to each
other]

catechumens something about the subtlety of temptation—and right as the Lenten struggle in the wilderness is beginning.

The recurrent refrain of the Word the catechumens have heard is that God alone is Meaning of all, God alone is to be worshipped; its melody continually returns to who human beings are before God—those rescued by His saving power—and that the appropriate response to that is worship. The catechumens heard that Jesus would set their minds free from their oppression by the Spirit of their Age, so that they can find Meaning in God and worship Him, and are free to love one another in truth. And now they must decide to whom they will turn for Meaning in their lives—to the Loving Truth, God revealed in Jesus Christ; or to the Spirit of their Age? Whom will they cherish over all? Will they worship God, or Satan? Do they want to call on this Jesus and leave an existence dominated by meaninglessness and alienation for a life governed by gratitude and acts of love? For if they call on Him, they cannot call on their own terms; when He rescues them from meaninglessness, this does not mean He will give them meaning according to their own limited and selfishly determined definition. The catechumens think of the hard bondage the Deceiver has laid on them, of the choice between the sterile futility of their slavery to him and the fruitfulness of a free life in God's Spirit. They will renounce their allegiance to the Spirit of their Age, they decide, and call on Jesus as the saving Lord who will rescue them from oppression and enable them to stay free of it.

But first the Faithful must make sure that the catechumens have had sufficient training to develop the stamina of spirit needed for the Lenten testing now ahead for all. Have they listened to the Word these many months as it was proclaimed to them? Have they walked by it and thus stayed on faith's journey's path? Have they sought the companionship of their guides on the way, have they prayed with them in the assembly which constitutes them as who they are?

The sponsors have given their consent; now the catechumens are asked for theirs. Do you wish to escape the dominion of the Father of Lies, and worship the Father of Mercy as His beloved child? Do you wish to be freed from sin's manacles of self-worship, which keep you from extending your hands to serve others or raising them to make offering to God in adoration? "Since you have already heard the call of Christ, you must now express your response to that call clearly and in the presence of the whole Church. Therefore, do you wish to enter fully into the life of the Church through the sacraments of Baptism, Confirmation, and the Eucharist?" The catechumens think how accustomed they are to their deadly No, of the struggle of letting it be

RCIA 131B

John 8:44
2 Cor 1:3

RCIA 132

Gal 5:24   crucified with Christ so He can raise them with His Yes; they think
of the wonder of His outstretched arm that would lead them through
mighty waters into a place of milk and honey, from slavery's starva-
tion from meaning to a rich harvest of gratitude. "We do," they say.

The names of the Elect are proclaimed and, as always, the Faithful
RCIA 134,   provision them by their prayer, this time requesting for them the spe-
135   cial equipment they will need for the Lenten trial ahead. "My dear Elect,
RCIA 136   you have set out with us on the road that leads to the glory of Easter.
Christ will be your way, your truth, and your life. Until we meet again
for the scrutinies, walk always in his peace."

As they gird themselves for the final stages of the journey, the newly
Elect know they are not alone. Those who have given them Word of
the One who will smash their shackles of unbelief and make them Faithful will be ever at their side. The Elect depart. Having begun this day
as aliens held in bondage, in forty days they will return, as strangers
Eph 2:19   no longer but fellow citizens with the saints at home in the worship
of God.

Summary: The Rite of Election and the Period of Purification and Enlightenment

The Rite of Election is the turning point in the rites of the catechumenate, for in this rite the converts pass from being those who have asked for faith and are preparing and hoping to be numbered among the Faithful, to being those the Church has chosen to baptize in the near future. Since Christianity is about converting, the Rite of Election marks the point when the community discerns that the catechumens have made sufficient progress in learning how to convert to sustain a lifetime of converting, so that they are capable of receiving the gift of the indwelling Spirit who will bring that conversion about, and will not receive the grace of God in vain. This is why the community must discern in those it elects conversion in mind and action, sufficient knowledge of Christian teaching and a spirit of faith and charity, and why those still trapped in patterns of serious sin cannot be elected. The rite itself gives ritual expression to the candidates' progress in conversion, both by announcing to the worshipping community that the principal signs of conversion are manifest in them (they have listened to the Word of God and attempted to shape their lives by it, and have joined in the fellowship and prayer of the whole community), and by allowing them to bear witness to the desire grace has wrought in them for salvation in Christ through the sacraments of initiation into the Church. The Rite of Election thus gives ritual articulation both to the theological reality of God's election, or call, of the candidates as seen in the transformation of their lives, and to their faith-experience of hearing that call and responding to it by giving their names for Baptism. In declaring their election, the celebrant charges the Elect to allow the work of conversion to deepen in them still more, so that they will be able to receive the fullness of salvation which God will begin to work in their lives at Baptism. The rite thus both expresses and, as the Spirit works through its proper readings and prayers, mediates the grace of conversion necessary for Baptism.

While the Rite of Election thus celebrates God's work of conversion taking place in the lives of the catechumens, the rite also bears witness that the community of faith is the essential matrix in which this conversion comes to fruition. The homily is directed to the baptized as well as to the catechumens, to encourage the Faithful to be shining examples in their own ongoing transformation through Christ's death and resurrection and thus to "accompany the elect along the path of the paschal mystery." At the Rite of Election, the members of the community who have been chosen to help the Elect through the final stages of yielding to grace necessary to prepare for Baptism, the god-

2 Cor 6:1

RCIA 120

RCIA 131, 132

RCIA 129

RCIA 123   parents, exercise this ministry publicly for the first time. It is in the
RCIA 125   name of the Church that the celebrant admits the catechumens as Elect.
The entire community joins in interceding for the Elect that they may
experience a deeper turning to God in the ways evoked by the procla-
mation of the Word, and, "after the election, they should surround the
Elect with prayer, so that the entire Church will accompany and lead
RCIA 121   them to encounter Christ."

     The Rite of Election thus celebrates the election of the candidates
in the larger context of God's election of a People, His choosing and call-
1 Pet 2:9   ing them that they may proclaim the wonderful deeds of the One who
called them out of darkness into His marvelous light; in the readings
and homily the Faithful are making that proclamation, so that those
who listen will be drawn through hearing it into the salvation the readings proclaim. Thus, even as the ritual gestures and prayers of the Rite
of Election both express what is actually happening between God, the
converts, and the community, and provide a vehicle for entering more
deeply into it, so do the three sets of readings proper to the rite. As
the Elect are committing themselves to be baptized and to undergo whatever final preparation the Faithful see as necessary, and the Faithful
are committing themselves to prepare and baptize them, the readings
provide the framework within which these commitments can be understood and lived.

     The final time of preparation for Baptism is centered on the Elect's
RCIA 139   coming to a deeper knowledge of Christ as Savior, and the proper readings for Election begin this process. Both the celebration of the Rite
of Election and the First Sunday of Lent (when this rite normally takes
place) call for preaching on the readings which centers on Christ as Savior of humankind from its oppression by sin, death, and Satan; the
celebration of Christ's victory at Easter or Baptism is meaningless unless those celebrating understand what He conquered and have experienced His victory in their own lives. The Elect, especially, need a
deeper understanding of what it is Christ is saving them from in order
to surrender to Him the areas of their lives in which they are oppressed
so that they can receive His salvation. Perhaps they did not think much
about sin, death, or hell before they became catechumens; it is a human
characteristic not to face problems for which one can see no solutions.
During their many months in the catechumenate, as they reflected on
their lives in light of the Gospel with the support of the community,
the converts could begin to perceive the depths of sin, the horror of
death, and the weight of spiritual oppression from which they need
to be delivered; their final preparation focusses even more intensely
on the meaning of the salvation Christ offers, for, to the extent that

they see their need of a Savior and truly desire one, to that extent are they able to receive His salvation.

In order to proclaim God's action to save which is at the heart of the Rite of Election, the Faithful continue, through the readings, to tell the story of how they have experienced Him saving them; the preaching on the readings seeks to draw the hearers into contact both with God and with the community in its relationship to God. The main difference between the three sets of readings that may be used for the Rite of Election is the specific point in the journey of God's people where the candidates for election are taken aboard; the history of God's saving relationship with His People is being recounted and the catechumens are being grafted into it. The readings also work together to provide the candidates with a language with which to speak of God's salvation and their own incipient experience of it. Whether they hear of the Fall (A), or the Flood (B), or the People's explanation of their family history, what has made them who they are (C), as the would-be Faithful are allowed to overhear God's conversation with His People before they were born and with His Faithful now, they are becoming increasingly familiar with the grammar of faith with which they would speak their lives. All three sets of Scripture readings for the Rite of Election, as all the proper readings of the RCIA, are full of images of God, of those seeking Baptism, and of the distance between them that must be negotiated through conversion. The psalms for the Rite of Election provide models of how to pray, as if the Faithful, in the intonation of the psalm refrain, were saying to the converts: "This is how God's People respond to Him—now you try."

Even as the readings seek to draw the candidates into a deeper conversion by proclaiming God's power to save, and providing language with which the Elect will be able to reflect on what is happening to them, they are also frank that coming into God's salvific will for their lives will not be without struggle. In all three sets of readings the Gospel is one of the synoptic accounts of Jesus' temptation in the desert; all three note that it was the Spirit who led Jesus into the wilderness to be tried by Satan and thus prove His Sonship. The catechumens have probably already been exorcised prior to the Rite of Election; it is appropriate for them to begin the final stage of preparation (during which they will be three times exorcised in the presence of the Church) with the reminder that both they and the Faithful are involved in a struggle

Eph 6:12   with more than flesh and blood.

The temptation accounts are also appropriate for the Rite of Election because, in celebrating God's salvation in Christ, the community is celebrating God's faithfulness revealed in Christ's obedience, and the

Gospel narratives bring this out clearly. The Gospel thus provides those who would be Faithful with a model of faithfulness for their Lenten preparation; as Abram, leaving his home for a new life God had promised, was the icon for the catechumenate, so Jesus tried in the wilderness is for the Elect. Regardless of which Gospel account is proclaimed, several lessons concerning faithfulness in temptation are offered to those entering the Lenten time of testing; since living a faithful life involves a deeper and deeper victory over temptation, it is fitting that the Elect begin to learn these lessons now, even in their final stage of intense spiritual preparation. The temptation Gospels warn the candidates not to be naive, not to think they can come to a deeper commitment to God without experiencing trial of their faith and love. They must learn that there is no shame in being tempted (only in giving in) because Jesus, the pioneer and perfector of their faith has been there first: He, too, fasted and was hungry; He, too, was tried. The Elect, too, will find their sonship questioned by temptation and must be sure of their identity, yet they must also learn that being child of God does not give them the prerogative of ignoring God's will in order to exalt or prove themselves; they must simply seek God's call for their lives and be willing to follow it, trusting that whatever it is, it is what will best enable them to know God's love and minister it in this life and the next. As catechumens the Elect learned to overcome temptation to obvious evil; now, like Jesus in the desert, they must learn to overcome temptation to apparent good: to value nothing, no matter how good in itself, over God's will for them.

Heb 12:2

The closer the Elect come to Baptism, the more resistance they may encounter; they need to become increasingly more aware of their Adversary's strategy of cheating them out of living as children of God and of the need to resist it. The temptation accounts can be read as confronting them with the Deceiver's ideas of how to approach material possessions, human relationships, and power, and with the contrasting ideas of a faithful Son; during the time of purification ahead they will come to see what their own ideas are. They will discover that idolatry is as serious a problem in Western culture as in any Third World "mission" country, and perhaps more dangerous, since the service of individualistic self-fulfillment is so taken for granted by the culture that it may not be recognized for the idolatry it is. They must face the fact that the way most human beings exercise power, including themselves, is not submitted to God's authority. They must clearly recognize that God is what is of greatest worth, and that the only way they can have the self-worth they crave is if their worth is based on His, conferred by Him.

The Gospel also warns them not to tempt God, to try to make Him prove what He has said is true, as if His Word were not trustworthy and needed to be proved; from Jesus' response to Satan's suggestions beginning *"If* you are the Son of God," the Elect can learn that any such proposition that calls into question what God has revealed as true (e.g., "If God really loved you") should not be followed to its conclusion, for that is surely as false as its premise. The Elect's process of learning to be Faithful is the process of learning on an even deeper level to say Yes to God, but the Deceiver's lies make this seem complicated, make it seem that they must qualify their Yes to His love because His love cannot really be trusted. Jesus' response shows the Elect that they must resist making conditions for God and actively struggle against their desire to be their own gods. If they allow Him, He himself will form in them the Yes they will speak with their lives at Baptism, as well as provide them with the armor they need for spiritual combat and, ultimately, give them the victory.

Deut 10:11   The temptation Gospel serves to warn the candidates that the land they have come to is not like the one they left: wild beasts, not to mention angels and Satan himself, inhabit it; it thus brings into sharpest possible focus the choice between opposite extremes that the converts have become increasingly aware of throughout the rites of the catechumenate. Through the Gospel at the Rite of Election the Faithful
Didache I, 1   say, as they have from the beginning, "There are two ways, one of life and one of death; and between the two there is a great difference,"
Isa 30:21   and urge, as they point to Christ, "this is the way; walk in it."

RCIA 138   The Gospel thus introduces the candidates into the territory they will find themselves in during the forty days to come, a time of purification and enlightenment. The Church wants its members to be realists, so as the Faithful are embarking on forty days of fasting in the wilderness where they will struggle with the mystery of evil and its effects in their lives, they invite the Elect to come with them, to be prepared for Baptism. Lent is a time when the Faithful and the Elect share the tension between the already and the not yet, for as the Elect are both in the Church, and yet on the way to being Church, so the Church is both the kingdom and on the way to being the kingdom. For both Faithful and Elect, a central temptation is to settle into an outward appearance of a faithful life, rather than allowing faith to reshape their lives. The Spirit of their Age continually badgers them to "be reasonable" and not really change direction or priorities; as long as they avoid anything seriously wrong, other than that they can please themselves: just be nice and try not to hurt anyone unless it's really necessary. Both Elect and Faithful must wrestle with external Christianity, and seek to give themselves as fully to God as they can at this stage in their lives; God will reveal to each person what this means for them now, and never asks more than is possible.

The Elect have long since discovered the influence of their No to God in their lives; in this final time of preparation they must face how fiercely alive and real it is, how weak they are when confronted by its power. "If you come forward to serve the Lord," the Faithful warn them, "prepare yourself for an ordeal"; the period of purification and enlightenment is for the Elect a time of discovering how *un*faithful they are, and this is good because it humbles them and enables them to seek the grace to change and learn to be Faithful. As they grapple with temptations to value possessions, relationships, control, more than love of God, to rely on them for salvation, they will see how vulnerable they are to not trusting God, and the extent to which their No still dominates them; they will also be humiliated as they discover the self-righteousness that mars the purity of their faith, the many subtle forms of self-justification they had unconsciously assumed would purchase for them Christ's saving Yes which can only be had as gift. In these changes of self-perception that humble them by revealing to them that they are not the center of the universe, the Faithful must encourage the Elect to be patient, perhaps reminding them that if gold, which perishes, must be tried by fire to be made pure and shine, so must their faith, far more precious and imperishable, be purified by trial. The impurities in the Elect's faithfulness—their Yes to the God who is Love—must be revealed, and they must be willing to yield them to Love's consuming fire. The furnace of humiliation will refine their experiential trust that God forgives sins and saves in time of affliction; it will teach them that as they work out their salvation in fear and trembling, God Himself is working salvation in them—for as is His majesty, so also is His mercy.

But purification is not the only aspect of the intense spiritual preparation of the Elect; the blazing fire to which they have come which would melt away their weaknesses and purify their strengths would also illumine their minds with a deeper understanding of Christ as Savior. The most precious truth there is, is the infinite love of God poured out to save in Jesus Christ, and the Deceiver will do anything to prevent people from knowing and believing that truth. For the rest of their lives the Elect will be facing temptation to abandon it, if not consciously, then practically: by not reflecting on it and letting something other than God's love in Christ determine how they think and behave, how they spend their time, energy, and material resources, letting it have the place only the Gospel should have; it is thus crucial that experiential knowledge of Christ as Savior begins to become the central reality of their

Sir 2:1

Sir 2:4

Sir 2:5
1 Pet 1:7

Heb 12:29
Sir 2:5, 11
Phil 2:12-13
Sir 2:18

RCIA 139

lives. Whereas the Elect have already seen much change in their behavior through what they have done (one learns to feed the hungry by volunteering in a soup kitchen, not by meditating about poverty), there is also a real need for an even deeper inner transformation to change their perception, and make them more open to the many dimensions of salvation God is working in them. Yet in seeking this enlightenment, as in seeking purification, the Elect are not trying to attain an abstract perfection, much less to earn the graces given at the font; *Didache* I, 1 their very desire to choose the "way of Life" by giving their names for Baptism is inspired by the Spirit, who also gives them the ability to follow it. The period of purification and enlightenment is thus a time when the Elect seek to learn on a deeper level what they have sought all along: to live in obedience to the Holy Spirit.

Yet the RCIA understands this conversion to living by the Spirit not as a private decision made by individuals for "personal reasons," but as the assimilation of those called by grace to die and rise with Christ in the community of faith where that Paschal Mystery is lived; and the heart of the community's living out of the Paschal Mystery is the worshipping assembly. Since the community of the redeemed are appointed to praise, it is at worship that they are most who they were Eph 1:12 intended to be, most truly themselves; since in beholding the glory of 2 Cor 3:18 God, they are transformed into His likeness from glory to glory, the worshipping assembly is a time of privileged encounter. It is in their time of communal trustful praising and listening, thus coming before God in filial obedience, that the community is united to the life of Christ and thus enabled to be a channel for the divine compassion in works of mercy outside the time of worship; transformation in Christ is therefore not a purely individual process but a communal phenomenon.

Thus, since it is at worship that human beings are most open to God, most in touch with reality, and since the Elect in their final time RCIA of preparation need a particularly strong dose of reality, the Church 141–148 provides the rites of the scrutinies and presentations as a source for the purification and enlightenment they need. In these rites, in addition to their ritual actions (laying on of hands, exorcism, presentations, etc.), the Church—Faithful and Elect—are called together to hear the Word and, by the Spirit, to allow it to become flesh in them, as a People, as well as in their individual lives. In the final time of preparation for Baptism, then, beginning with the Rite of Election, the readings of the rites play a vital role in the Elect's purification and enlightenment; as always they are catalyst for the Elect's transformation into the new identity they began to journey toward when they became catechumens. The readings for the Rite of Election have painted for the converts vivid

portraits through which they can understand how far they have come:
from those who rebelled, to the perfect number of the elect. Thus, even
as the final stage of the journey begins, the Faithful offer the pilgrims,
instead of a map, a maelstrom of images that serve as a murky cloud
by day and an often-terrifying pillar of fire by night—by which they
themselves are guided.

Exod
13:21-22

III. The First Scrutiny

"The scrutinies, which are solemnly celebrated on Sundays and are reinforced by an exorcism, are rites for self-searching and repentance and have above all a spiritual purpose. The scrutinies are meant to uncover, then heal all that is weak, defective, or sinful in the hearts of the elect; to bring out, then strengthen all that is upright, strong, and good. For the scrutinies are celebrated in order to deliver the elect from the power of sin and Satan, to protect them against temptation, and to give them strength in Christ, who is the way, the truth, and the life. These rites, therefore, should complete the conversion of the elect and deepen their resolve to hold fast to Christ and to carry out their decision to love God above all" (no. 141).

RCIA	*Lectionary, Third Sunday of Lent, A*
nos. 7, 9, 20, 30, 138-146, 150-156	Exod 17:3-7 Ps 95:1-2, 6-7abc, 7d-9 Rom 5:1-2, 5-8 John 4:5-42

As those long married might return to the place where they first
learned to love each other, so the Church each year returns to the place
of her betrothal, the wilderness, and seeks to renew her commitment
to the One who made her holy bride, to allow her love to be purified
and grow deeper. And when the Faithful followed that One their soul
longs for into the desert at the Gospel of the First Sunday of Lent, they
brought the Elect with them to learn the lessons of betrothal, and come
to know the steadfast love of the One to whom they will be joined,
who morning by morning gives them bread in the wilderness. But
though the Elect have seen how faithfully He provides the bread of His
Word to feed their hunger, they are not sure that is enough.

Only two weeks have they been here? How can it be?—it seems
forever. Last year, when they were catechumens, they had been so im-
pressed as they watched the Elect at these Scrutinies. How wonderful
it must be, they had thought, to *finally* be chosen for Baptism, to have
the Faithful say, you are ready to be bearer of that Love that gives us
our life as children of God. How wonderfully humble and holy they
seemed, last year's Elect, as they listened to the Scripture so attentively,
and knelt so reverently for prayer! How powerful it must be to feel
the whole congregation praying for you, to feel the loving pressure of
your godparents' hands, to feel the awesome words of exorcism pierc-
ing through you! To be "Elect"—God's chosen one—to have everything
in your life going so well, to feel so close to God, how wonderful it
must be!

But now they themselves are Elect, and it is not that way at all:
everything in their lives is not going well and they certainly don't feel
close to God. Oh, the bread of the Word that comes each day has been
all right, but one gets tired of its sameness. And this Lenten wilderness
is so dry. God seems so far away. And they are so thirsty. Where is
God anyhow? This is not at all what they expected. God is supposed
to be taking care of them, meeting all their needs—and making them
feel holy and full of peace and joy.

And the Faithful act as if nothing were wrong, as if this were normal! Why did they bring us here—so we could watch our spirits shrivel
up and die? At least before we followed them we were safe from this:
we put "number one" first and took care of our own needs. We placed
our trust in nothing, we had no expectations, our hearts were firmly
closed—we couldn't be disappointed . . . Why did you bring us here?
You told us there was a God who loved and cared for us—but we don't
see it. We listened to you, we opened our hearts to trust, and now,
exposed in this arid waste, our hearts can parch and wither. We are
so thirsty, we can't think of anything else. We have had just about
enough of this. Why did you bring us here? Where is this God you

Hos 2:14-20

"The
Church's
One
Foundation,"
S. Stone

Ps 42:1
(Songs 3)

Lam 3:22-23
Exod 16:4,
21

Num 11:6

say you follow—is He real or not? If He is real, why can't we feel His love? Why isn't He taking care of us? Where is He?

The lector opens the Book and the Faithful return to their story.

> At Rephidim the people thirsted for water, and the people murmured against Moses, and said, "Why did you bring us up out of Egypt, to kill us and our children and our cattle with thirst?"
>
> So Moses cried to the LORD, "What shall I do with this people? They are almost ready to stone me."
>
> And the LORD said to Moses, "Pass on before the people, taking with you some of the elders of Israel; and take in your hand the rod with which you struck the Nile, and go. Behold, I will stand before you there on the rock at Horeb; and you shall strike the rock, and water shall come out of it, that the people may drink."
>
> And Moses did so, in the sight of the elders of Israel. And he called the name of the place Massah and Meribah, because of the fault-finding of the children of Israel, and because they put the LORD to the proof by saying, "Is the LORD among us or not?"

Exod 17:3-7

The Elect are startled by the profusion of images that now gush forth from the Book before them. They immediately discern the clear picture of God as standing before His People, able to work wonders to help them, giving them to drink even when they turn from Him in rebellion and put Him to the test; He is source of the water that every creature needs to live. They also find it easy to distinguish the images of themselves: thirsty, murmuring against their leader and God, ready to find fault with Him and put Him to the test. The Faithful, they perceive at first, come to them as Moses, guiding them away from their bondage to sin, demonstrating to them that God does provide—but there is more to it than that.

"We have been where you are," the Faithful say, "and God has brought us through, as He quenched the thirst of our forebears in the desert. But they've told us their story as warning to us as well as you; so we always return to the wilderness to listen to His Word, to seek to let it penetrate our lives yet more deeply. What those before us have written for our instruction is what we pass on to you: When they found themselves in dire need on their pilgrimage, they complained instead of trusting, and put God to the test—and He met their need as He would have met it had they not tried Him. But they found that though they gained the water they murmured for, they lost a far more precious source of life: by testing God they cut themselves off from pleasing Him, and made themselves unable to live in the land of His loving promise. They were overthrown in the wilderness and left their story to their children as a warning."

1 Cor 10:6

1 Cor 10:11

1 Cor 10:5

The Faithful thus tell the story of where they have come from and what they have learned from it to admonish themselves as well as the Elect. For although they have progressed further on faith's journey, at times they, too, can find they are focussing on what they don't have and think they need, rather than on God's care, and murmuring that He has left them thirsty. From their forebears the Faithful have learned that to act thus is to refuse to trust God, and to turn away from living in love with Him; one cannot be in loving relationship with someone one doesn't trust.

Like the Elect, the Faithful have seen that while God has promised to supply their needs, it sometimes seems that He has not; but they have learned that this is because His understanding of their needs is different from their own and that, knowing all, He knows their true needs as they never can. Unlike them, He knows their future path and what they will need to walk it; unlike them, He knows what will best prepare them to live in perfect love with Him forever. He has shown the Faithful that when they see there is something they lack and find fault with Him, they are putting their faith in their own determination of what is good for them, rather than in His unbounded care, worshipping themselves instead of the only One who can give them the salvation that is what they truly need.

The Elect must decide, and the Faithful decide more deeply, that God's understanding of their needs is the true one. They must want Him and the salvation He offers them above all else—above all their ideas of what will make them happy, whether it be circumstances in their lives or spiritual consolation: their ideas of "being holy" or what being holy feels like are not necessarily God's ideas and may not even be good for them. They must decide that *He* will be their portion; they will find that He is good to those who seek Him, waiting quietly in hope for His salvation. If they are going to live as His children, they must believe their Father knows their need before they ask, and, when they find they lack something, approach Him as one approaches a loving Father, trusting He will give them whatever they truly need to know His love.

Lam 3:25-26

Matt 6:8

It is to learn this trust that God ever brings His people to the wilderness. Here the Elect will find, as their teachers have already discovered, that no matter how difficult the trial that may tempt them to doubt His care, the Faithful One will not let them be tempted beyond their strength; with the trial He will always give them means of escape and, as they trust Him, will work all things together for good.

1 Cor 10:13

Rom 8:28

As the images stream from the Book open before them, the Elect find themselves somewhere between the doubting People and trusting Moses, somewhere between thirst and water. They hear those who have

gone before them warning them, if they would live in loving relationship with God, not to be like those who complained He deserted them
before they even asked for His help; for to be Faithful means to trust
His faithfulness.

"And he called the name of the place Massah and Meribah, because
of the fault-finding of the children of Israel, and because they put the
Lord to the proof by saying, 'Is the Lord among us or not?'" They must
trust, the Elect decide, but what does this mean in practice? "Show us,"
they ask the Faithful; "if we must not approach the God who brought
us here with murmuring, show us what it looks like to approach Him
as those who trust." But the cantor has already begun.

Ps 95:7d-8a   R̸ If today you hear his voice, harden not your hearts.

O come, let us sing to the Lord;
    let us make a joyful noise to the rock of our salvation!
Let us come into his presence with thanksgiving;
    let us make a joyful noise to him with songs of praise!

O come, let us worship and bow down,
    let us kneel before the Lord our Maker!
For he is our God,
    and we are the people of his pasture,
    and the sheep of his hand.

O that today you would hearken to his voice!
    Harden not your hearts as at Meribah,
    as on that day at Massah in the wilderness,
when your fathers tested me,

Ps 95:1-2,   and put me to the proof, though they had seen my work.
6-7abc, 7d-9

As the cascade of images of their condition continues, the Elect find
it begins to quench their thirst. God is immediately recognizable as the
One who is solid as a rock and thus worthy of their trust to bring them
salvation. More than that, it was He who made them, who cares and
works for them as a shepherd providing for His flock, speaking to them,
calling them by name; He is to be adored and greatly praised. The Faithful, the Elect see, are the People who belong to this God, the sheep
whom He leads to the pasture He provides to feed them. Above all,
they are God's worshippers who make a joyful noise praising Him with
thanksgiving, singing to the One who rescues and redeems them.

Yet the Faithful know that they must not allow themselves to become arrogant because of this identity. They heard the first reading,
they know that their forebears who had seen God part the Red Sea
for them and feed them on manna from heaven still refused to trust
Him, and put Him to the proof; the Faithful know that if they think

1 Cor 10:12   they now stand above such behavior, they had better take heed lest they fall. Thus in the psalm they are exhorting the Elect as well as themselves that they cannot deny that they have heard God call them, so they must not harden their hearts from trusting Him.

   The Elect see that they are being called to identify with this cared-for flock, this People who have been given salvation and forever respond with loud praise. To those who had begun this day complaining and wondering where God was, the Faithful proclaim that His presence is entered with thanksgiving, and call the Elect to come with them as they give thanks and come before Him. The Elect had asked what trust looks like in practice, and in the psalm the Faithful show them by entering into worship, for the trust that they seek begins with worship. The Faithul demonstrate that this worship is not a matter of fulfilling a requirement of reeling off a few prescribed sentences once a week, but is a gift of their entire selves, by singing of how the whole body is involved: bowing down, kneeling, singing, making joyful noise. As the Elect make this gift of self, expressed in worship, they will begin to trust. Warned by the example of those who went before, they will

Phil 4:6   learn to bring their needs to God with thanksgiving, rather than anxiously avoiding Him and finding fault; they will learn to praise Him

1 Thess 5:18   in all circumstances.

   Set before them the Elect see, on the one hand, those who harden their hearts and put God to the proof, and, on the other, those whose very existence is to praise God for the salvation He gives. In answer to their desire to know what it means to approach God in trust, the Faithful have invited the Elect to become worshippers and instructed them in how to praise. The Faithful have also reminded them that they *have* heard God's call and exhorted them to listen to Him, and not to close and harden their hearts to Him and put Him to the test. *Today* is their chance to hear His voice, to make the choice they must each day renew to be a worshipper and not a murmurer; *today* is their chance to obey, to open themselves to the grace that will work their redemption.

   "If today you hear His voice, harden not your hearts." They *have* heard His voice, and the very act of singing the refrain has made them desire to keep their hearts open, but still they must know more, think the Elect. What keeps their hearts from drying up as they try to live

1 Cor 10:4   a life of praise? And what is the mysterious rock from which they quench their thirst on their journey, that some have said will follow them through the wilderness?

     Since we are justified by faith, we have peace with God through our Lord Jesus Christ. Through him we have obtained access to this grace in which we stand, and we rejoice in our hope of sharing the glory of God. And hope does not disappoint us, because God's love has been poured into our hearts through the Holy Spirit who has been given to us.

While we were yet helpless, at the right time Christ died for the ungodly. Why, one will hardly die for a righteous man—though perhaps for a good man one will dare even to die. But God shows his love for us in that while we were yet sinners Christ died for us.

Rom 5:1-2, 5-8

The Faithful have shown the Elect that a life lived in right relationship to God is a life of self-giving trust that expresses itself in worship. Yet even though the Elect would like to give themselves to God this way, they have long since found they cannot generate this trustful relationship by their own striving, so they ask the Faithful to explain the source of their worshipful trust toward God that makes them acceptable to Him. Always ready to give an account of the hope that is in them, the Faithful now set forth their answer.

1 Pet 3:15

Only One of their kind, the Faithful explain, could of Himself offer perfect trust and worship to God; and by living this perfect love, even to the death it cost Him, He made up for their rebellion: His life of perfect praise drowned out their murmuring, and won for them the grace of being in right relationship with God. Christ now offers to His kind the trust He lived, and those who accept it are thus made acceptable to God; through Christ they know, not strife, but peace with God, and are able to stand before Him in worshipful trust. And not only can they stand in His presence and trustfully adore Him in this life— they rejoice because they expect they will praise Him yet more perfectly with His own glory, in the life that never ends.

And if at times the Faithful find themselves wondering at the awesomeness of such an expectation, they remind themselves of how they know that it is true. For when they were rebellious and could not come to God in loving trust, God came to them and gave His Son to death so they could trust; a God who loves like that will give them life in love with Him forever. And more—they know eternal loving praise is what He destines for them because already He has given the down payment. His own love poured into human hearts keeps their hearts from drying out, and ever overflows to sing His glory; a God who pours His love into them now so lavishly, will give them life in love with Him forever.

As they listen to the Faithful's explanation of how their Lord Jesus Christ is the source of that worshipful trust toward God which they seek, the Elect know the Faithful are describing to them the grace of Baptism for which they are preparing. It is this faith the Faithful describe—not just intellectual assent to concepts but a trustful commitment of their lives to God—which is what makes them righteous, what justifies them, before Him; and God Himself would give them the trust they need to be acceptable to Him. For while they are yet helplessly trapped in their murmuring, and have no power to worship God trustfully as sons, the Son who offered perfect worship would breathe into them His own Spirit—the Spirit of His Sonship—so they can live in trust and praise forever.

Through the epistle the Faithful have reminded the Elect of their condition, and allowed them to be confronted by the stark contrast between ungodly sinners and those who are at peace with God, filled with the Holy Spirit and hope of endless glory. By pointing out how rare it is for someone to die even for a good person, they have called the Elect to remember the cost of their redemption and reflect more deeply on God's astounding love for them in Christ.

The Elect are not sure what to think. They have heard this all before, of course; if the epistle were broken up into propositions on a True/False test, the Elect are certain they would pass it. But the Faithful don't present the reading as helpful religious concepts, but proclaim it as ultimate reality and Truth. They talk about this Father as if they were His sons, about this Jesus as if they knew Him, about this Spirit as if they experienced His love flowing through them. Where do they get such confidence to speak like that? And is their dazzling hope of endless glory really posible *for us?*—how can we *know* that it is true—who will show us?

"But God shows His love for us in that while we were yet sinners, Christ died for us." The Faithful recall when they, too, asked these questions, and know that there is only One who can answer them. "Return with us to the source from which we draw our wisdom; see if there you meet what you are looking for."

John 4:42, 15   ℣ Lord, you are truly the Savior of the world;
give me living water that I may never thirst again.

Jesus came to a city of Samaria, called Sychar, near the field that Jacob gave to his son Joseph. Jacob's well was there, and so Jesus, wearied as he was with his journey, sat down beside the well. It was about the sixth hour.

There came a woman of Samaria to draw water. Jesus said to her, "Give me a drink." For his disciples had gone away into the city to buy food.

The Samaritan woman said to him, "How is it that you, a Jew, ask a drink of me, a woman of Samaria?" For Jews have no dealings with Samaritans. Jesus answered her, "If you knew the gift of God, and who it is that is saying to you, 'Give me a drink,' you would have asked him and he would have given you living water."

The woman said to him, "Sir you have nothing to draw with, and the well is deep; where do you get that living water? Are you greater than our father Jacob, who gave us the well, and drank from it himself, and his sons, and his cattle?"

Jesus said to her, "Every one who drinks from this water will thirst again, but whoever drinks of the water that I shall give him will never thirst; the water that I shall give him will become in him a spring of water welling up to eternal life."

The woman said to him, "Sir, give me this water, that I may not thirst, nor come here to draw."

Jesus said to her, "Go, call your husband, and come here."

The woman answered him, "I have no husband."

Jesus said to her, "You are right in saying, 'I have no husband'; for you have had five husbands, and he whom you now have is not your husband; this you said truly."

The woman said to him, "Sir, I perceive that you are a prophet. Our fathers worshiped on this mountain; and you say that in Jerusalem is the place where men ought to worship."

Jesus said to her, "Woman, believe me, the hour is coming when neither on this mountain nor in Jerusalem will you worship the Father. You worship what you do not know; we worship what we know, for salvation is from the Jews. But the hour is coming, and now is, when true worshipers will worship the Father in spirit and truth, for such the Father seeks to worship him. God is spirit, and those who worship him must worship in spirit and truth."

The woman said to him, "I know that Messiah is coming (he who is called Christ); when he comes, he will show us all things."

Jesus said to her, "I who speak to you am he."

Just then his disciples came. They marvelled that he was talking with a woman, but none said, "What do you wish?" or, "Why are you talking with her?"

So the woman left her water jar, and went away into the city, and said to the people, "Come, see a man who told me all that I ever did. Can this be the Christ?" They went out of the city and were coming to him.

Meanwhile the disciples besought him, saying, "Rabbi, eat." But he said to them, "I have food to eat of which you do not know."

So the disciples said to one another, "Has anyone brought him food?"

Jesus said to them, "My food is to do the will of him who sent me, and to accomplish his work. Do you not say, 'There are yet four months, then comes the harvest'? I tell you, lift up your eyes, and see how the fields are already white for harvest. He who reaps receives wages, and gathers fruit for eternal life, so that sower and reaper may rejoice together. For here the saying holds true, 'One sows, and another reaps.'

I sent you to reap that for which you did not labor; others have labored, and you have entered into their labor."

Many Samaritans from that city believed in him because of the woman's testimony, "He told me all that I ever did."

So when the Samaritans came to him, they asked him to stay with them; and he stayed there two days. And many more believed because of his word. They said to the woman, "It is no longer because of your words that we believe, for we have heard for ourselves, and we know that this is indeed the Savior of the world."

John 4:5-42

In the epistle the Faithful have provided the Elect with the information that the source of their relationship of trust and worship to God is Jesus, but the Elect need to know whether this is true for *them.* Are the Faithful well meaning but self-deluded, or is Jesus truly a living person who is offering them a relationship of love with the ultimate power of the cosmos—to which their only possible response is to surrender their whole lives forever? In the end, only Jesus Himself can answer that for anyone. At the Rite of Acceptance into the Order of Catechumens, the Faithful sought to introduce the Elect to Him, but it is rare for a person to give their life to someone else completely when they have just met; so as the Faithful have continued to bring the converts into His presence in the Gospel proclaimed, they have prayed that through it He will reveal Himself to them.

John 1:35

"How can we know if Jesus really offers us what the Faithful say?" the Elect are wondering, and as the Gospel begins they think back over all that has happened since they first encountered Him. It had started so innocuously—one ordinary day, a day like any other, the kind of day you can't even say a week later what you did that day, they had been going about their normal business, going to meet some need, to keep things together till the next day. And somehow He got mixed up in it; how He happened to show up in that place at that time they could never quite figure out later, but there He was seeking their attention. They tried to dismiss Him lightly—really, how could He expect them to show any interest in Him, they were not the religious type, you know, they were well-adjusted modern people .

Then suddenly—how, they were never sure—their interaction took a quantum leap, and He was telling them He could give them some kind of living water. They humored Him and asked Him where He got it, stalling for time as they planned their getaway from this increasingly embarrassing encounter. And then He answered them quite seriously that if they drank this water He gave them, it was so potent that they wouldn't need to continually wear themselves out running around, trying to keep it all together till the next day; they would never thirst, in this life or ever. "Sure," they had said, trying to make a graceful escape, and coolly gave their parting shot, "Well, thanks a lot, I'll have to try some sometime."

But then He showed them—how had it ever happened?—that somehow He knew everything about them, even things they tried to keep themselves from knowing because they didn't want to face them. And even more than that, unlike they who had lived through all the events of their lives, *He* understood those events, knew what they all meant; as He explained things to them they began to see for the first time in their lives everything that had ever happened to them fitting together into a plan, which started somewhere and went somewhere and actually made sense. And where it went was to Him. It was wonderful and terrifying—perhaps there was a God somewhere who really understood them, and He had some connection to that God. But this didn't answer everything.

If He had some special kind of hot line to God (how else could He show them how their whole life made sense when even *they* had never seen it?) then, they asked, what did God—distant, isolated, wind-up-the-universe-like-a-clock-and-let-it-run God, expect from people as worship? What were the right words to repeat, ceremonies to get through, so they could do the right thing and get it over with? That was missing the point, He had told them. The God they thought isolated had come near, as near as their own flesh, so they could know Him, and any true worship was rooted in the truth of that gift of Himself; it was even more intimate than that, for God in His own Spirit could indwell them and unite them to Himself in praise. And then He told them who He was, and they knew, somehow they just knew, that it was true; the day before they hadn't known, but now they did. He was sent by God, chosen by God, to make things right. The news was so good they could hardly believe it, but they rushed off to tell those they loved the most . . .

Oh yes, the Elect think, yes, we saw, He showed us that He was the One God had chosen, His Anointed, the Christ—and we believed Him, we never would have made it this far otherwise—and we *have* tried to give our lives to Him: get rid of sin, help those in need; but as we listen to the Faithful tell their story at this scrutiny, we hear them calling us to something more, to a trustful worship which is a deeper gift of ourselves. They're telling us, "It's not enough to say, 'Yes, we have decided to join those who think that Jesus is God's chosen'; to be baptized you must give yourself to Him as source of your existence, stop trying to sustain yourself with anything less, thirst after Him alone, and come to know Him as your Living Water."

Can we do this? What would it mean, to let Him be the water that sustains us, rather than all our plans for self-actualization? . . . As the Elect consider this, they find bits and snatches of things they have heard the Faithful say over the many months begin to come together in their minds with what they hear today; the answer seems to fall into two parts.

✓ To accept Him as Living Water in their lives is to be willing to trust Him completely for all they need to live. While of course they must always seek after what is good (as He guides), when something does not go well they must not let it cause them to turn away from Him in selfish anger—for then they are letting it be more important to them than He. If He is their Living Water, if His love is what's most impor-

1 Thess 5:18   tant, they will give thanks in all circumstances, because His love is con-
Rom 5:3-4   stant and ever deserves their praise; even in adversity they will rejoice, for it increases their hope in the glory to come, and the hope He gives them is sure. They must entrust their ambitions for happiness into His care, and accept all He allows to come to them with praise; He is greater

Rom 8:28   than any turn of events they encounter, and can work them all for good. To know Him as Living Water is to know him as Redeemer ever pouring forth His love to wash them from their false worship of self, which but for Him would bring them death; and to let this be the true source of their happiness. Then, no matter what trial overtakes them, they

Rom 8:18   can offer trustful praise, for it is not worth comparing to His love endlessly cascading to cleanse them, undeserving: the only source of joy that endures forever. If He is their Living Water, their thoughts will stream with gratitude.

And overflow with mercy. That is the second part, they see. For if their own difficulties should inspire them to trust and praise, the difficulties of others beckon them to service. Those who are flooded with the Living Water of unbounded mercy must not only praise but

Mercy   be merciful and generous in turn: forgiving those who wrong them, giving to those in need. As the divine compassion flows through them, they are to be channels of it to others, bringing the presence of Christ into every situation in which they find themselves. This, the Elect see, is how one would live if one knew Christ as Living Water.

Can *we* do this? Can we live our lives this way? How can we do it? The Elect stand uncertain at the well of the Word where the Faithful have brought them. How can we make ourselves know Christ as Living Water, so we can live in trust and praise and service?

"You can't—for I reveal myself, I give myself, as gift to those who ask. That is why my People brought you here today: so you could hear me asking you to ask. I am the Living Water, welling up now in those who ask me, with the trusting praise and love that lasts forever. Let me show you all the ways you murmur after things that can never quench your thirst; bring them to me so I can wash them away and

give you to drink of my Spirit of life. Take me at my Word and let
Luke 11:9   me be Living Water for you. Only ask, and I will give; only come to
John 7:37-39 me and drink, and out of your heart will flow rivers of love and praise."

As they hear Christ speaking to them through the Gospel, the Elect
find their questions answered; they know where the Faithful get their
confidence, and they know that they too are offered—not just a life
of respectable churchgoing—but a Spirit of endless glory. They also
see the task before them to prepare for the coming of this Spirit. Part
RCIA 141 of the purpose of the scrutinies is to uncover and then heal what is weak,
defective, or sinful in their hearts; as the Elect reflect on the areas of
murmuring (of ingratitude for His salvation, of rebelliously refusing
to entrust themselves to God), in their lives, they are helped by the
pairs of opposites in the Gospel: thirst, and living water that those who
drink will never thirst again; worship limited by human constraints,
and true worship in spirit and truth; knowledge acquired through another, and knowing by personal experience.

The Faithful also, who would have listened to these readings whether
the Elect were there or not, recall the sheer grace by which they, too,
with the Samaritan woman and now the Elect, came to know Jesus as
God's Anointed, and consider how faithful they have been to their acceptance of His offer to be the Living Water of their lives; they are so-
bered by His saying to them that what sustains Him is to do His Father's
will. If they had begun to be rather proud of themselves for planting
the faith in the Elect, who have come so far and are almost ready for
reaping, the Faithful hear Him remind them that *He* sowed the desire
for Life in their hearts; their Easter harvest will be the fruit of His gift.
More, if the Faithful cannot claim credit for converting the Elect, neither should they try to bolster their own egos by keeping the converts
always dependent on them as spiritual authorities, mediators of their
relationship to God. The Elect must believe—as their own converts must
someday believe—not only because the Faithful are such good teachers,
but because they have heard the Teacher Himself, and come to know
Him, experience Him, as Savior.

"They said to the woman, 'It is no longer because of your words
that we believe, for we have heard for ourselves, and we know that
[Relationship this is indeed the Savior of the world.'" In the deep silence after the
of readings homily, the Elect reflect on what has happened to them since they en-
to each tered the assembly this day. As they were grumbling at their lack of
other] consolation, the reader opened the Book, and they were inundated with
God's answer in life-giving images. In the Old Testament lesson they
were confronted with the apparent absence of God, in the psalm they
learned to enter His presence with thanksgiving, in the epistle they were
promised access to God through Christ, in the Gospel they heard where

and how God chooses to be present, and met Him in Jesus, the One He sent. They saw God providing life-sustaining water to rebellious Israel, the love of God poured into the hearts of sinners, and the living water promised those who ask. God was the rock of their salvation, they heard, and Christ the Living Water bursting forth to save them; because of what He did they can have grace and know that they will see God's glory. They have heard that the Father seeks those who worship Him in spirit and truth, that worship is thus not external duty but the heart of a love relationship with God. Yet if adoring God for who He is, is at the heart of Christian life, He gives His Spirit to make it possible; as the Elect open their lives to this Spirit, their lives will be channels of God's love for others.

[Rite and faith-experience]

RCIA 141

The Faithful know that as the Elect consider what they have heard, they will find themselves drawn more than ever to enter into the life of the Faithful, for the scrutinies are intended to "complete the conversion of the Elect and deepen their resolve to hold fast to Christ and to carry out their decision to love God above all"; and the scrutinies do this as the Spirit works through the readings, prayers, and exorcisms to challenge the Elect to a deeper surrender of their lives to God, show them what that means, and empower them to do it. At the Rite of Acceptance into the Order of Catechumens the converts were called to a new identity, and during the catechumenate they steadily journeyed toward this transformation of their personalities. Now in the scrutinies this new identity comes into even sharper focus, as they perceive more clearly what it would mean in their daily lives and the obstacles against it; each scrutiny allows them to name in their own hearts the obstacles the Spirit reveals to them, and ask the community's intercession for the grace to abandon them.

RCIA 152

As the presider calls them forward for silent prayer, the Elect think back on what this scrutiny has laid bare. Part of its purpose was to bring out and strengthen what is good, and if the Elect are honest, they can see much good: they have heard the Lord's voice, and don't deny it or decide to harden their hearts against it; they are willing to listen as He shows them new ways that they must learn to trust; they are willing to learn a deeper kind of praise. Yet the scrutiny has also uncovered much in them that must be healed. They have seen that the mystery of sin, of human rebellion against God, is deeper than they had thought, and that they participate in it in all the ways they refuse to entrust themselves to Him; as they perceive their need for purification and redemption is greater than they had known, they find they desire it more.

RCIA 152

"Elect of God, kneel down and pray." In the psalm the Faithful invited them to express the reverence in their hearts with their whole selves, and now they do. They want to turn from their vain thirst and drink of His life-giving Spirit; during this time of silent prayer they bring to Him their murmuring and ask Him to help them trust. "If you but knew the gift of God. . ." they hear Him say. "Lord, give me this water," they answer, "that I may never thirst again."

John 4:10
John 4:15

The Faithful do not know the specific areas for repentance the scrutiny has revealed to each of the Elect, but they do know from experience the basic needs of all preparing for Baptism, so they seal the time of silent prayer with their communal intercessions. They have told the Elect they have been given their lives to give glory to God and service to others, but they will only be able to do this inasmuch as they know Christ as Living Water; the Faithful join in petitioning for them all the graces that will lead them to this knowledge.

RCIA 153

But while the Faithful have been empowered to ask in confidence, they have also been given the authority to do more: in Christ's name they can call down release from any bondage that keeps the Elect from entering into the freedom of the children of God. "God of power . . ." As the Elect hear the words their minds are filled with the mighty acts of God throughout all history. Their doubts of His care seem further away and a new strength stirs within them, a deeper promise that they will be faithful to Him, come what may. "Lord Jesus . . ." they hear, and think in their hearts, "You are the fountain we long for. We will take You at Your Word. Spring up within us to life everlasting and overflow to the thirsty." ". . . for you live and reign forever and ever." "Yes, we will trust You to be our Living Water." "Amen."

Rom 8:21
RCIA 154

John 7:38;
4:14

As the Elect open their eyes and prepare to be dismissed they realize that this final time of purification and enlightenment is, like the rest of the catechumenate before it, a land of promises and warnings. At this first scrutiny they have been warned: at the Rite of Election they were told not to put God to the test once they had entered the wilderness; now they are reminded that although leaving the seeming security of slavery to sin is difficult and they may want to doubt God's presence at thirsty times, they must nevertheless keep journeying toward God's absolute sovereignty over their lives—their chance to obey is *today*. They are promised access to God, His love, His Spirit.

Matt 4:7

"Dear Elect, go in peace, and join us again at the next scrutiny. May the Lord remain with you always."

"Amen," and they depart. They came this day demanding earthly waters, but left—their water-jar abandoned—turning in trust to Christ the Redeemer as Living Water.

John 4:28

IV. The Presentation of the Creed

". . . Thus, with the catechumenal formation of the elect completed, the Church lovingly entrusts to them the Creed and the Lord's Prayer, the ancient texts that have always been regarded as expressing the heart of the Church's faith and prayer. These texts are presented in order to enlighten the elect. The Creed, as it recalls the wonderful deeds of God for the salvation of the human race, suffuses the vision of the elect with the sure light of faith" (no. 147).

RCIA	*Lectionary*
nos. 21, 138–139, 147–149, 157–162	Deut 6:1-7
	Ps 19:8, 9, 10, 11
	1 Cor 15:1-8a
	(or Rom 10:8-13; see Rite of Election, C)
	Matt 16:13-18
	(or John 12:44-50)

Exod 17:1-3   Just a few days ago the Elect stood here murmuring loudly with
the People who went through this desert before them, but God preserved
the People, and they moved on to a further stage on their wilderness
journey; and today the Elect find that the People's descendants have
brought them along to this later point on the journey, so they can learn
its lessons, too. Unlike the last time they came together, today the Elect
have not come eager to complain that God's providence for their lives
is not tailored to their self-centered specifications. Their thoughts are
still dominated by their encounter at the well; "Yes, be my Living
Water," they keep finding themselves thinking. But what exactly does
it mean that Christ would be their Living Water? They caught a glimpse
of it on Sunday, but the reality of living one's everyday life with Christ
as Living Water is so deep that it cannot be fully assimilated in one
liturgy or one encounter with Christ. And what will enable them to
live this life of trusting praise and service that depends on Christ as
its source, day by day for years and years after they are baptized? They
know the Faithful have probably told them before, but they need to
hear it again, or maybe said a slightly different way; they want something more to think about, to give articulation to the graced desire they
find welling up in them to know Christ as Living Water.

So today they have not come with demands, but are eager to listen, recalling how many times the Faithful have opened the Book to
them and given them exactly what they needed. As the reader begins,
the Elect strain to catch every word.

> Moses said to the people: "This is the commandment, the statutes
> and the ordinances which the LORD your God commanded me to teach
> you, that you may do them in the land to which you are going over,
> to possess it; that you may fear the LORD your God, you and your son
> and your son's son, by keeping all his statutes and commandments, which
> I command you, all the days of your life; and that your days may be
> prolonged. Hear therefore, O Israel, and be careful to do them; that it
> may go well with you, and that you may multiply greatly, as the LORD,
> the God of your fathers, has promised you, in a land flowing with milk
> and honey.
>
> "Hear, O Israel: The LORD our God is one Lord; and you shall love
> the LORD your God with all your heart, and with all your soul, and with
> all your might. And these words which I command you this day shall
> be upon your heart; and you shall teach them diligently to your chil-
> dren, and shall talk of them when you sit in your house, and when you
> walk by the way, and when you lie down, and when you rise."

Deut 6:1-7

As Moses before them, the Faithful proclaim what God has revealed,
and the Elect recognize certain familiar images that help bring their de-

sire into focus. They are reminded of the mystery that the God they are beginning to perceive more vividly in His coming to them as Savior in Christ—whom they yearn to know as Living Water—is One; and that this One God is to be feared—honored—and obeyed over all. He does not leave them futilely struggling to ascertain on their own what He is like and how creatures can honor and obey Him, but *reveals* Himself and His loving will. He is Giver of Commandments, of the way by which His People are to live in the place He would give them so that they can grow in this land of plenty as He has promised.

As they listen, the Elect realize that the Faithful are imaged in this reading not only as Moses, but as the People to whom God has given a way to live, a promised life abundantly nourished with the milk and honey of Word and Sacrament. The Elect recognize themselves as those who listen, with Israel, to hear what God will speak that they must live by, and see that they are becoming part of a long line of those who have had God's Word entrusted to them. They are on their way to the Promised Land, where their lives must be formed by God's life-giving revelation so that they can receive the new life He would give them there and prosper in it. And in order for their lives to be formed by what God has revealed—by His Word—they must allow Him to engrave it on their hearts; they must let His Word saturate their being, so that they can teach it to their children and constantly think and speak of it: at morning and evening, at home and abroad. For the new existence God would give them is rooted in loving Him with their whole heart, soul, and strength, and it is in allowing themselves to be so penetrated by His Word that they will be able to live out that love.

As the Elect find themselves drawn into Moses' proclamation to God's People, they consider how these words speak to the needs they brought to the assembly this day. The Faithful had urged them to desire to know God in Christ as Living Water, as source of their existence, and Christ Himself had told them He would give Himself as Living Water to all who asked. But how, the Elect had been wondering, how could they cooperate with His coming, what was *their* grace-given part in allowing Him to give Himself to them this way? Now, as they listen to God's servant Moses and his heirs, they see where they can begin. To be able to live with God in Christ as their Living Water, they must resolve even more deeply to love Him over all else, and live out this resolution by dedicating themselves to cherishing His Word. As catechumens they learned to value His Word, and tried to walk by it, yet it was for them a distant standard outside of them, by which they must measure themselves. Now the Lord asks them to allow Him to write His Word, His understanding of reality—the only true

understanding—on their hearts; they must commit themselves on a yet
deeper level to basing their lives on what He has revealed, His Word.

As the Faithful hand on what God has spoken, they are also, as
always, reminding themselves not to stray from the life that has been
given to them: they will only be able to teach God's Word "diligently"
to the Elect if they too continually reflect on it and speak of it, if they
too dedicate themselves to loving God with their whole being. "Be care-
ful," they warn the Elect, and exhort themselves as well: "When you
have entered the life He promised, don't forget who brought you there;
with your whole being revere and love Him and no other. Don't try
Him as you did at Meribah, but be Faithful to what He reveals to you.
And when those for whom you are given responsibility, ask you why
you live your life the way you do, tell them of the God whose awesome love has freed you from sin's bondage; tell them of the new life
He has given you, and how it is ruled by the power of His saving Word."

"And these words which I command you this day shall be upon
your heart; and you shall teach them diligently to your children, and
shall talk of them when you sit in your house, and when you walk
by the way, and when you lie down, and when you rise." The Elect
are reassured that even though they could not say exactly what it was
they needed, the Faithful seem to understand. Those to be baptized need
to know more about how to conduct themselves in the new land they
are coming to; the Faithful have called them to hear God's Word to
them and live by it, so they can receive the life of abundance God has
promised. The Elect, of course, had heard this before (as they had sus-
pected), but as the Faithful proclaimed it they were struck with how
extraordinary it is that God should speak to humankind, reveal Himself to them; they felt in themselves a deeper appreciation for God's
gift of revelation that brings them life, a deeper desire to join with the
Faithful in grounding their lives in praise for this gift.

Deut 6:10-25

John 6:68   ℟ Lord, you have the words of everlasting life.

The law of the Lord is perfect,
        reviving the soul;
the testimony of the Lord is sure,
        making wise the simple.

The precepts of the Lord are right,
        rejoicing the heart;
the commandment of the Lord is pure,
        enlightening the eyes.

The fear of the Lord is clean,
        enduring forever;

the ordinances of the Lord are true,
and righteous altogether.

More to be desired are they than gold,
even much fine gold;
sweeter also than honey
and drippings of the honeycomb.

Ps 19:8, 9,
10, 11
(RSV, Ps
19:7, 8, 9,
10)

As Israel gives thanks for God's gift of the Law, the Elect join their voices in praising the same God who speaks to them, too, for what He speaks gives them life forever. In the verses of the psalm the Faithful, whose lives are permeated with gratitude for God's Word, bear witness to the truth of what God is like. What He commands them is perfect, giving life to the dead; the Way He gives them to walk is utterly secure. What He teaches them is righteous and pure, illumining their perception and giving them wisdom; to hear such truth brings joy to their hearts.

As they join in the Faithful's song of celebration of God's saving revelation, the Elect perceive that coming into the Church is entering into the Church's deep love for God's Word, His Way, and living by it. That God would give Himself to them as He does in revealing Himself—this is sweeter than the most delectable thing human beings can crave; it alone can satisfy forever. The Elect see they must treasure what God reveals more than any shining wealth, for living in awe of His Word will keep them forever from the stain of deadly sin. As the Elect in praying the psalm affirm the power of God's Word—everlasting life—with the Faithful, who have had years to know this power in a deeper existential way, they find their own conviction in that power growing deeper. The Lord's Word will transform their whole being, they realize: their mind, their heart, their soul, their vision.

The Elect have come this day as the simple, needing wisdom and the light and joy only God's Word can bring. The Faithful, who try to absorb the Word of God in every way, all the time, and have gone further in knowing who God is, share their knowledge in praise as well as proclamation. "Lord, you have the words of everlasting life." But the Faithful know they must do more than exhort the Elect to cherish God's Word and lead them in praise. If the Elect are to continue living out a life of praising God for speaking to them a Word that saves, a life of seeking to be formed by His Word so they can love Him, they must be absolutely clear on the heart of that Word: His most intimate revelation of Himself. The reader turns the pages of the Book as if saying to the Elect, "We have heard Moses set us on the right path; now listen with us to our brother Paul."

I would remind you, brethren, in what terms I preached to you the gospel, which you received, in which you stand, by which you are saved, if you hold it fast—unless you believed in vain.

For I delivered to you as of first importance what I also received, that Christ died for our sins in accordance with the scriptures, that he was buried, that he was raised on the third day in accordance with the scriptures, and that he appeared to Cephas, then to the twelve. Then he appeared to more than five hundred brethren at one time, most of whom are still alive, though some have fallen asleep. Then he appeared to James, then to all the apostles. Last of all, he appeared also to me.

1 Cor
15:1-8a

With Paul, the Faithful preach the message entrusted to them, reminding the Elect with urgency of this good news of greater value than any created thing: "You have heard that you must let God write His Word on your heart, and form your very being; the core of that Word is what He has revealed about Himself. He is Keeper of Promises; what He once spoke—we know He spoke it for those who went before us wrote it down—He has fulfilled: His Christ has died for our sins, been buried and raised for our justification. Christ is Risen Lord who saves; He is the hinge of human history. For what we tell you is not comforting symbolic myth but fact. Christ conquered sin and death in power, He revealed His reign, there are witnesses: Peter, the Twelve, and hundreds more, and Paul—and we ourselves! This is the living heart of what God has told us about Himself, this is the heart of what you give yourself to at Baptism, the basis of your new existence: the redeeming death and resurrection of Jesus Christ, the Son of the Living God; this good news will save you if you hold it fast."

This, too, they have heard before, think the Elect; hearing this message is what brought them to this assembly in the first place. Yet they realize as they listen that the Faithful are showing them that, with the people of Corinth (and the Faithful themselves), they need to hear it again: that this gospel is not something they can master in one hearing and then move on to other things. Each day they must remind themselves of it, proclaim it to themselves; and each time they truly hear it they learn something new, for the depths of God's mercy in Christ cannot be fathomed.

food for the journey!

The Faithful, then, are not repeating what the Elect already know, but are seeking to lead them to deeper enlightenment; for of all that they can preach to the Elect, the truth that Jesus Christ is Lord who died and rose to forgive their sin is of first importance, and the Elect must understand this clearly if they are to continue on their journey to the font. So the Faithful hand on the gospel that they themselves received, insisting with those who handed it on to them that this good news is authentic: it was foretold, confirmed by testimony of witnesses, preserved, and carefully passed on. As so many times before, the Elect realize that what is happening in their lives this day has become a mirror image of what the Faithful are proclaiming through the Scriptures. As Paul bears witness to the truth of Christ's revealing Himself as saving Lord to those before him and "also to me," so do the Faithful; and the Elect are receiving this gospel, learning to stand in it, hearing it will save them if they are faithful to it; they find themselves confronted with the opposite extremes of holding this gospel fast and being saved, and believing in vain.

"Last of all, he appeared also to me." The Faithful have made it clear: this gospel of Jesus Christ as redeeming Lord is the Word the Elect must let God write on their hearts, so that it informs every aspect of their lives. But the Elect must do more than simply nod their agreement and they know it. "This saving truth more precious than all else, how do we hold it fast? We have come to your assembly, we have learned the things you taught us, we have worked with you in serving those in need—what else must happen for us to be saved by this Word?" The Elect sense that they need not only to know on a deeper level that this gospel itself is true as statement of a concept, but also need a deeper experiential knowledge that it is true for them personally. The Faithful, to whom Christ has been revealed as saving Lord (as they just bore witness), know that this deeper knowledge is possible, but that it is not theirs to give; "one greater than Moses" is needed. As the deacon carries the Gospel Book to the ambo, he holds it high, as if raising a giant burning-glass to catch the Spirit's rays and focus them on the Elect.

John 3:16

℣ God loved the world so much, he gave us his only Son,
   that all who believe in him might have eternal life.

When Jesus came into the district of Caesarea Philippi, he asked his disciples, "Who do men say that the Son of man is?"
   And they said, "Some say John the Baptist, others say Elijah, and others Jeremiah or one of the prophets."
   He said to them, "But who do you say that I am?"
   Simon Peter replied, "You are the Christ, the Son of the living God."
   And Jesus answered him, "Blessed are you, Simon Bar-Jona! For flesh and blood has not revealed this to you, but my Father who is in heaven. And I tell you, you are Peter, and on this rock I will build my church, and the powers of death will not prevail against it."

Matt
16:13-18

He is standing right in front of them; He speaks matter-of-factly, as if they were in the middle of a conversation. "The people you know, the people that you work with every day, your teachers when you were in school, your government leaders—what do they say about me?"

It has been a while since the Elect thought about this, they have been so absorbed in their own journey; slowly, thinking while they answer: "Well, that you're a teacher—maybe a great one, like Buddha or Mohammed. Deluded about a lot of things, but with some good ideas; basically, a good man, well, as good a man as any. Someone you can take or leave, you know, whatever makes you feel good."

His very presence before them confronts them with the question that comes next; evenly but with intensity: "And you—what do you say?"

They take a breath to rattle off an answer they memorized long ago, but then they stop, suddenly absolutely certain that this is no longer enough; the answer He seeks must come from a deeper level in them— but they see the implications and they hesitate. And yet they can go no further on their journey without answering, for He is blocking their path; to go on they must somehow go through Him, through the question His presence to them embodies.

But the Gospel burning-glass has done its work; the Spirit's flame has seared the answer on their hearts. "You are" (and they know it is true), "You are the Son of the Living God, the one anointed by the Father to give your life for us to save us. You are the pearl beyond all price, for which we must forsake all else; You are the Lord."

They wonder at the strength of their conviction: when they came to the assembly this day they were disciples who had been following Jesus for some time; they had thought they were as committed as they could ever be. But the Faithful knew there was more to discipleship than the Elect had yet discovered, so they brought them in this Gospel to Jesus, so He could put to them the only truly important question ever asked of them; having instructed the Elect in the first reading to base their lives on God's Word, the Faithful brought them to encounter the Word-made-flesh, so the Father could send His Spirit to reveal who Jesus is "also to them": that He died for *their* sins, that He is *their* Risen Lord. For the Faithful know this saving confession and its living out in the one who was first graced to make it is the foundation of their life as a People, which the Elect are seeking to become part of; and as the Elect, by their own personal affirmation, allow themselves to be built on this foundation of Jesus Christ as Saving Lord, He Himself will build them into a temple of living stones, unconquerable by death.

The Elect are awed by the greatness of what God is doing for them. Nothing they could have done, nothing even the Faithful could have done, could have given them this conviction, enabled them to recognize this truth on which all reality is based. Only God could have showed them this—and He cared enough to show it to them and call them to be built into His People He frees from death! The Faithful, too,

Matt 13:46

1 Pet 2:4-5

"So high as well might go in at the door."

as they see the fire of saving faith enkindled in the Elect, are also awed, remembering when they first came to know the Lord as who He is, realizing anew what a sheer gift that recognition was, and, with Peter and the Elect, affirming their confession.

"How can we hold fast to the good news you proclaim?" the Elect had asked, and now they see: by accepting the revelation God has made to them of Jesus Christ as *their* Redeeming Lord, and confessing it, and accepting it as the foundation on which they will be built together with all those who also entrust themselves to the foundation of this saving confession. The Elect see that through the Word, as always, the Faithful have been guiding them on their journey between pairs of opposites: what people say, and what *they* say; flesh and blood, and their Father in heaven; the powers of death, and the Church which prevails over them.

"And Jesus answered him, 'Blessed are you, Simon Bar-Jona! For flesh and blood has not revealed this to you, but my Father who is in heaven. And I tell you, you are Peter, and on this rock I will build my church, and the powers of death shall not prevail against it.' This is the Gospel of the Lord." And the deacon is holding out to them a gleaming pearl.

Matt 13:46
[Relationship of readings to each other]

As the readings come to a close, the Elect consider where the Faithful have brought them through these Scriptures. "Live by the Word," they had said in the first reading, and then in the epistle that Word was no longer laws to obey but a precious truth to cherish. "Live by the Word," the Faithful had said, and in the Gospel that precious truth is a Person to love and confess. So the most intimate heart of what God has done and been for them, of what He speaks to them, is the reality that Jesus Christ is their Redeeming Lord; and for them to allow God to write this saving Word on their hearts is to allow His Spirit to make Christ's death and resurrection active in their lives, forming in them the character of Jesus. But this means they must protect this precious truth, they must not lose it in over-preoccupation with other things or confusion. They look to the Faithful: "You have offered us your pearl beyond all price—but how can we keep it safe? Is there a treasure chest where we can lock it for safekeeping?"

"We would not hide the priceless jewel of the gospel out of sight. We have set it in a diadem of links of gold forged by the Spirit to protect it and show off its dazzling light. Come, we will show you the Spirit's craftsmanship."

RCIA 160

"Let the Elect now come forward to receive the Creed from the Church." And as they file up to where the presider waits, they sense that he is not alone. For those who mined the Scriptures for the gold in this crown, who fashioned it as guided by the Spirit, and all who shed their blood for it, and all who lovingly proclaimed its links and faithfully passed it down—all these, too, are present when the Faith is handed on.

"My dear friends, listen carefully to the words of that faith by which you will be justified. The words are few, but the mysteries they contain are great. Receive them with a sincere heart and be faithful to them."

"We believe in one God. . ." says Moses, says Israel; "We believe in one God. . ." repeats the Church.

Athanasius,
*Orationes
contra
Arianos*

". . . We believe in one Lord, Jesus Christ . . . one in being with the Father . . ." says Athanasius, say the Fathers of Nicea; ". . . one in being with the Father," echo the Faithful. And then they proclaim all the facts of what this God actually did when, incarnate, He was

Cyril of
Jerusalem,
Catechesis
IV, 9

part of human history, saying by their tone of voice: this is not a useful set of symbols, but the framework of all reality; if this is fantasy, then so is our salvation.

Basil, *On
The Holy
Spirit*

". . . We believe in the Holy Spirit, the Lord, the giver of life. . . . With the Father and the Son he is worshipped and glorified . . ." says Basil, say the Fathers of Constantinople. "With the Father and the Son he is worshipped and glorified," affirm the Faithful.

". . . We acknowledge one baptism for the forgiveness of sins. We look for the resurrection of the dead and the life of the world to come," say the baptized of all the ages, thousands upon thousands of ordinary people like the Elect, whose names are now forgotten on earth, but who live and are named by God; who through two millennia kept this crown of faith burnished bright by their lives and so ever come as witnesses when it is yet again passed on. ". . . We look for the resurrection of the dead and the life of the world to come," confess the Faithful.

This is the Church's Creed; the whole church delivers it: all in the assembly present it to the Elect by proclaiming it aloud, joining in the confession of the unseen witnesses who delivered it to them. As the Faithful have held out the diadem to the Elect, turning it slowly so they can see the perfect design of each link, the Elect see clearly how this crown has set the luminous truth of the saving Lordship of Jesus Christ to greatest effect. "Keep your mind within the circlet of our Triune faith, within the golden mysteries of what God has done; let these shining truths ever frame your thoughts, and then you will keep safe our radiant pearl."

The Elect gaze on this crown, knowing that they have heard the statements of the Creed many times, that they learned about each one in the catechumenate, but today they see them for what they truly are, as links forming together a whole crown, in which each separate link is necessary. They perceive that if they understand what has been proclaimed, it will not be hard for them to memorize, for each part calls out for the others, each link leads naturally to the next.

[Relationship of rite and faith-experience]
And as the Elect contemplate this crown, the Faithful reflect on how it is the best gift they could have given them today. The Elect had come brimming with inarticulable longing to live with God in Christ as their Living Water, as source of their existence. But the Faithful know that this desire which increasingly surges up in the Elect must be channelled if it is to reach its goal, and not spend itself spilling out in all directions at once in self-indulgent enthusiasm. The Faithful have learned that the desire for a life of love of God and service is safeguarded by fidelity to God's Word, the truths of what God has revealed of Himself in history; and so to safely channel the Elect's graced desire the Faithful have shared with them their forebears' articulations of those truths in the Creed. As the Elect continually repeat these precious truths to themselves as they memorize the Creed, their amorphous longing to know God in Christ as Living Water will be shaped by the truths of who that God really is and the awesome destiny He has given humankind, and will thus be enabled to reach its goal.

[Relationship of readings and rite]
And in this Presentation of the Creed, as in all the rites, the readings and the ritual action are combined as an inseparable whole in expressing and mediating the Elect's growing in faith. In the Old Testament lesson the Faithful exhort the Elect to love God over all and, in order to do this, to revere His Word to them; in the Presentation of the Creed they offer the Elect God's Word spelled out in human words to guide them in understanding what He has revealed. "Lord, you have the words of everlasting life," sing the Elect in the psalm, and those "words" are the proclamation of Jesus Christ as Redeeming Lord which is protected in the Creed. As the Faithful share with the Elect the giving of the Old Law in the first reading, in giving them the Creed they share with them the New Law in Christ, the truths God spoke for all time in the Word-made-flesh, which are more to be desired than gold and sweeter than honey; in joining in the psalm refrain the Elect are hymning the precious truths of the Creed which are about to be presented to them, and their very acclamation in faith helps enable them to receive it. For there is a difference between hearing the Creed as a nonbeliever might, as a collection of declarative statements to be analyzed on the basis of other things, and receiving it as God's Word, the Living Truth that will shape and determine one's life forever; praising God for the "words of everlasting life" helps prepare the Elect to receive (not merely hear) those "words" in the Creed.

In the epistle the Faithful exhort the Elect always to remember the Redeeming Lordship of Jesus Christ and hold this good news fast so they can be saved; the Creed helps those who profess this, the heart of the Gospel, to hold onto their saving knowledge, and preserves its meaning so it is not distorted. Through Paul's insistent "that"s the Faithful emphasize that they are delivering facts which they themselves received: *that* Christ died, *that* He was raised, *that* He appeared. The God who saves is not an abstract theory; He has revealed Himself in history and the memory of His revelation is preserved in the Creed. As Paul calls upon the testimony of witnesses to confirm his gospel, so the Faithful in this rite are presenting the testimony of those who went before to the truths of the Creed in which that gospel is enshrined: Moses, the hundreds who saw the Risen Lord and Paul, Peter who confessed Him, and the Fathers of Nicea and Constantinople; perhaps the homilist has mentioned others through whose lives that testimony was passed on: Miriam, who saved Moses from death to hear God's Word; Mary, the first witness of the Resurrection; and Macrina, whose godly life persuaded her brother Basil to leave the pursuit of worldly success to seek the truth as the Church's servant.

Exod 2:7
Matt 28:1
Gregory of
Nyssa, *Life*
of Macrina

But merely hearing the testimony even of such impressive witnesses does not ensure that the Elect will actually *receive* the Creed the Faithful are delivering to them as their own possession. Being able to *own* that Faith involves a serious decision to believe; this is why the Faithful bring the Elect to Jesus in the Gospel, so He can ask them the question on which their life depends. Their recognition of Christ as Son of God who saved them enables them to receive the "mysteries" of the Creed "with a sincere heart and be faithful to them."

RCIA 160

Taken together, the readings prepare for the Church's solemn action in presenting the Creed by bearing witness to a God who has appeared and made Himself known, who keeps His promises: by the authority of this God, Jesus spoke; by the authority of Jesus, the Church speaks in delivering her saving confession. Through the readings the Church shows the Elect that they stand today on the threshold of the Promised Land, needing to know the law of that land so they can live there. The Church, a People saturated by a Word of infinite value and sweetness and saved by a Truth, urge the Elect to love that God over all—to be ruled by His Word: His saving work historically rooted in Jesus Christ and empowered by the Spirit—and crown them with reasons why.

RCIA 161

"Let us pray for the Elect. . . ."

But now the Elect need the Church's intercession, for in accepting the Creed they are accepting responsibility for the Church's faith, which they will meditate on as they memorize it, and be expected in a few weeks' time to profess publicly as their own.

". . . give them true knowledge, sure hope, and sound understanding, and make them worthy to receive the grace of baptism. We ask this through Christ our Lord. Amen."

RCIA 162

"Dear Elect, go in peace, and may the Lord remain with you always."

"Amen," and so they go. They came this day groping for words to express their longing for God; they leave bearing a golden diadem, whose links faithfully articulate the contours of their love.

V. The Second Scrutiny

"Because they are asking for the three sacraments of initiation, the elect must have the intention of achieving an intimate knowledge of Christ and his Church, and they are expected particularly to progress in genuine self-knowledge through serious examination of their lives and true repentance" (no. 142).

RCIA	*Lectionary, Fourth Sunday of Lent, A*
nos. 7, 9, 20, 30,	1 Sam 16:1b, 6-7, 10-13a
138–146, 164–170	Ps 23:1-3a, 3b-4, 5, 6
	Eph 5:8-14
	John 9:1-41

Seven Sundays on their journey's steep ascent from election to Easter, seven terraces where they can be strengthened by purifying instruction on their final climb to grace, and today they are halfway. Three weeks ago they pledged themselves to put their No to death, and three weeks from now they will drown it. At least that was the plan . . . All this language of living water and crowns and a life of everlasting love that last week was so full of—sure, it sounds good when you hear it. And when you're surrounded by the Faithful in the assembly it seems convincing: you can have a new life, things can be different, God has chosen you to give you a whole new life.

But then you go out and look at how things *really* are, and the Faithful's message is so unrealistic. Well, maybe it works for them, but it could never work for us. We could never really be holy, we can never really *know* God: we can't concentrate or even sit still to pray! "Rejoice in all circumstances," the Faithful said—face it, we're just not the joyful type. We could never really be holy: we're just not naturally generous; we have such a hard time just staying out of sin! The Faithful say God is calling us to reign with Him in glory—just look at us, we could never reign over anything! We just don't have what it takes to live this life of faith. Why did we think God chose us? Maybe it was pride; maybe we should back out before it's too late. Oh, we'll listen to your Word, we won't walk out and make a scene; but how could it have any Word from God for *us*?—anyone who looks at us can see we're not the kind of people He is looking for.

"Come with us," say the Faithful, patiently, "for on this Sunday we go to be with one who hears the voice of God. Come with us, and let us see what we can learn."

> The LORD said to Samuel, "Fill your horn with oil, and go; I will send you to Jesse the Bethlehemite, for I have provided for myself a king among his sons."
>
> When he came, he looked on Eliab and thought, "Surely the LORD's anointed is before him."
>
> But the LORD said to Samuel, "Do not look at his appearance or the height of his stature, because I have rejected him; for the LORD sees not as man sees; man looks on the outward appearance, but the LORD looks on the heart."
>
> And Jesse made seven of his sons pass before Samuel. And Samuel said to Jesse, "The LORD has not chosen these." And Samuel said to Jesse, "Are all your sons here?"
>
> And he said, "There remains yet the youngest, but behold, he is keeping the sheep."
>
> And Samuel said to Jesse, "Send and fetch him, for we will not sit down till he comes here."

And he sent, and brought him in. Now he was ruddy, and had beautiful eyes, and was handsome. And the LORD said, "Arise, anoint him; for this is he." Then Samuel took the horn of oil, and anointed him in the midst of his brothers, and the Spirit of the LORD came mightily upon David from that day forward.

1 Sam 16:1b,
6-7, 10-13a

The Elect recognize Samuel right away. They came to know him in the catechumenate—and how they admired this prophet who even

1 Sam 3:1-10 as a child was so keenly sensitive to the voice of God it woke him from sleep! Yet now the Faithful have invited them to witness how even one so close to God as Samuel could, by his own reasonable perception, be mistaken about who it is God chooses and why. The application is inescapable: if Samuel, evaluating a situation on the basis of his human vision unaided, could misperceive how God was acting, how much the more can the Elect! And they have even better cause for their mistaken view. For they have now come halfway on the final stage of their pilgrimage, and the closer they come to their destination, the more rugged the terrain looming before them, the more resistance they encounter within themselves. Baptism is no longer a pleasant fantasy of someday being holy, but an event only three weeks away. Considered at such close range, the prospect of being buried with Christ and then raised as a truly new person is, when they take it seriously, terrifying. It is easier to look for ways out: to look for indications proving that this death to all they have known can't really take place, and to call their heaping up of the many such indications "humility"—and then perhaps (with a secret sigh of relief) to feel sorry for themselves that they have gone to all this trouble preparing for something they were just never cut out for to begin with.

But the Lord told Samuel, and He told the Faithful, and He tells the Elect: He does not see things the way they do. And, like Samuel, the Church does listen carefully for God's true Word, and speaks it only after hearing it, to the Elect. By His Spirit who enlightens them, the Faithful have recognized God's choice of the Elect and reaffirm it to them through this scrutiny. No matter how things may appear judged by external evidence, the Lord knows everything about them, who they really are; He sees in the depths of their heart what is most true about them—the desire for Him—even if they do not at this moment, for He put it there. It is He who chooses whom He shall anoint with His Spirit, and He has chosen them.

For, He reminds them, *He* is the main character in the story they have been listening to these many months, and being grafted into as they listened. *He* decides whom He will call; *He* speaks and makes His call known, commissioning His servant who listens to anoint His chosen, consecrating His Elect for service to Him; and He sends His Spirit rushing on His anointed. Above all, *He,* and He alone, *sees*—sees *truly;* unlike humankind He sees not the superficial appearance of things but their inner reality.

Through His Word, the Faithful have continued to guide the Elect on their journey between opposite extremes: the way people see (outward appearance), and the way the Lord sees (the heart); those not chosen, and those chosen, anointed and given the Spirit. Carefully the Church has unsheathed the living sword which is the Word, and with its two-edged message laid bare their hearts: "Yes, though it may seem you are least likely for God's favor, you are indeed His chosen; if you endure with Him, you shall reign with Him, for He has summoned us to anoint you, and He will pour His Spirit mightily upon you from that day. But be aware your natural sight is not the way the Lord sees; don't evaluate what God is doing by your own vision. O Chosen of God, to live out your life in the way of those God has chosen, you must be willing to have your perception changed, be willing to see as He sees."

"Then Samuel took the horn of oil, and anointed him in the midst of his brothers; and the Spirit of the Lord came mightily upon David from that day forward."

Eph 6:17

Heb 4:12

2 Tim 2:12

Ps 23:1

℟ The Lord is my shepherd; there is nothing I shall want.

The Lord is my shepherd, I shall not want;
    He makes me lie down in green pastures.
He leads me beside still waters;
    He restores my soul.

He leads me in paths of righteousness
    for His name's sake.
Even though I walk through the valley of the shadow of death,
    I fear no evil;
for thou art with me;
    thy rod and thy staff,
    they comfort me.

Thou preparest a table before me
    in the presence of my enemies;
Thou anointest my head with oil,
    my cup overflows.

Surely goodness and mercy shall follow me
    all the days of my life;
and I shall dwell in the house of the Lord
    forever.

Ps 23:1-3a,
3b-4, 5, 6

In the first reading the Elect have witnessed the Lord's election of David; now David leads these whom the Lord has also called, in joining with him in his response to that call: the affirmation that faithfully living out the Lord's call is rooted in turning to Him and knowing Him as shepherd. As the Elect concentrate on following the Faithful in the notes of this refrain, the Faithful, through the cantor, sing with David this song they learned from him about what it means to be God's chosen, what one's life is like. They affirm that God truly does supply everything they need, even as a shepherd taking care of his flock: He leads them into the luxuriance of His living Word to sustain them, slakes their thirst with His Spirit; when they are weary He gives them rest and refreshes them, giving them peace, restoring their soul. To reveal that He is Truth which is all-powerful, He not only shows them the right way to live, but gives them the ability to follow it. And wherever He leads them, He stays with them there; because He is present with them in the most dangerous places, even when death's dark shadow towers up around them on all sides, there is no evil for them to fear: He is with them as Comforter. God is providing for them even when they are beset by their Adversary, preparing a banquet where He will give them to drink of the overbrimming chalice of His love, honor them with the precious perfume of His Spirit.

The Elect were familiar with these words from greeting cards they had seen even before they were catechumens, but as they listen to the cantor proclaim them today, they realize how, ultimately, they truly *are* utterly dependent and need to be led and cared for like sheep. They

Luke 12:32
1 Pet 5:2

see that the Faithful are describing to them their life as the flock of those God has chosen, the life in the Church for which they as Elect are preparing: a life spent in the lush pastures of God's Word, where He feeds them abundantly on what will best nourish them and where they drink of His baptismal forgiveness. The Faithful also sing of knowing God as host of a feast where He fills their cup to overflowing and anoints them with His Spirit—a feast to which the Elect are invited. This God promises protection to His own, and the Elect will find themselves always surrounded by His ever-forgiving love and gracious gifts; for to be in the Church is to be in His dwelling place, to begin a life of intimacy with Him now that will last forever.

"The Lord is my shepherd; there is nothing I shall want." The Faithful have borne witness to those God has chosen to join His flock that to live as His chosen they must come to know Him as shepherd, and have given them the opportunity to grow in this knowledge by expressing their trust in the all-caringness of God as they sing the refrain. But now that the Faithful have presented in greater depth the first part of the message of the first reading: that the Elect, with the Faithful, *are* God's chosen, that they *do* belong to Him and He will care for them, they turn to the second part: how God's chosen, Faithful and Elect, must change to live as part of His People.

> Once you were darkness, but now you are light in the Lord; walk as children of light (for the fruit of light is found in all that is good and right and true), and try to learn what is pleasing to the Lord. Take no part in the unfruitful works of darkness, but instead expose them. For it is a shame even to speak of the things that they do in secret; but when anything is exposed by the light it becomes visible, for anything that becomes visible is light. Therefore it is said, "Awake, O sleeper, and arise from the dead, and Christ shall give you light."

Eph 5:8-14

As the Elect hear this exhortation to the baptized—those at Ephesus and those who surround them in the assembly this day—to conduct themselves in a way that is faithful to God's choosing them in Baptism, they realize that the Faithful have invited them to listen in on God's Word to them this Fourth Sunday of Lent to give them a clearer understanding of the baptized life for which they are preparing. Having just borne witness through the psalm of how God cares for His chosen, the Faithful now consider how God's chosen live their lives in response. The Elect hear the Faithful addressed as children of the God-Who-Is-Light, who emerged luminous from the waters of their baptismal birth, and are admonished to live as what they are, for light gives birth to what is good, right, and true. While light is thus fruitful, darkness yields only works that are barren, so it issues in death, not life: those who harden their hearts to God, setting themselves up as gods in His place, have minds filled with this darkness; blinded by the ignorance of their futile self-worship, they stumble into every kind of deception, greed, anger, and filth, unable to see it for what it is. But when the Faithful were baptized into Christ who is Light of the World, He gave them the light of His Spirit who shows those who have come from this deadly darkness how to walk. Those united in Baptism to Christ the True Light must walk, as He does, the path of self-sacrificing love and forgiveness; they must ever allow His Spirit to illumine their minds so they can perceive the works of light prepared for them to walk in, and do them with thanksgiving.

1 John 1:5

Eph 4:17-19

John 1:9
Eph 4:32
Eph 2:10
Eph 5:4

Even while the Elect listen to the Faithful being exhorted to walk worthy of the calling to which they have been called, they know that they too are being instructed in the way they must walk to be worthy of God's choosing them in Baptism. The epistle reminds them that before they set out on this journey, they were indeed mired in the murk of self-worship and its shameful works, although they kept this hidden

Eph 4:1

Eph 4:18 in their darkened minds even from themselves. The Elect have come a long way now, but through this Word they perceive that in whatever ways their lives are yet apart from the God-Who-Is-Light, they are even today still in darkness, and His Word warns them to have nothing to do with its deadly works. How are they to heed this? With the Faithful, they hear, the Elect must allow God's light to reveal to them things as they really are: to expose the sin in them for what it is and, as they allow Him to uncover it, they must name it for the darkness it is and face the fact that it must be destroyed. For once the Elect are baptized, they must not walk as they did before they were enlightened, hiding in the darkness of self-worship, doing shameful things, but give their attention to how they can please God; as the Spirit's light

Eph 4:23-24 renews their minds, enabling them to see as God sees, this will make it possible for them to live according to their new nature, and they will be able to learn to walk as children of light, enfleshing in their lives (thoughts and actions) what is good, right, and true.

But today, the Elect realize, they are still somewhere between darkness and light, in the realm of shadows, where the dusk lulls them into lethargy; perhaps this is why they were losing sight of the fact that God had chosen them. "Wake up!" cry the Faithful, remembering when they first woke and resolving to be yet more alert; "Ask Christ our Light to show you whatever darkness you're still hiding, where you need the

Mal 4:2 Sun of Righteousness to shine." As always, the path they point out to the Elect lies between opposite extremes: people who do shameful things, and those who seek to please the Lord; the works of darkness done in secret, and the good, right, and true done visibly; the blind sleeper who is dead, and the awakened one who sees and arises to walk in the light.

"Awake, O sleeper, and arise from the dead, and Christ shall give you light." Struggling to rouse themselves, the Elect pull themselves to their feet to greet the Gospel. They think of how Jesus offered Himself to them as Living Water at the well, and as Redeeming Lord at Caesarea Philippi. Now they will ask Him for light, and they look eagerly for its golden brilliance.

John 8:12 ℣ I am the light of the world, says the Lord;
the one who follows me will have the light of life.

As Jesus passed by, he saw a man blind from his birth. And his disciples asked him, "Rabbi, who sinned, this man or his parents, that he was born blind?"

Jesus answered, "It was not that this man sinned, or his parents, but that the works of God might be made manifest in him. We must work the works of him who sent me, while it is day; night comes, when no

one can work. As long as I am in the world, I am the light of the world."
As he said this, he spat on the ground and made clay of the spittle and
anointed the man's eyes with the clay, saying to him, "Go, wash in the
pool of Siloam" (which means Sent). So he went and washed and came
back seeing.

The neighbors and those who had seen him before as a beggar, said,
"Is not this the man who used to sit and beg?" Some said, "It is he";
others said, "No, but he is like him."

He said, "I am the man."

They said to him, "Then how were your eyes opened?"

He answered, "The man called Jesus made clay and anointed my eyes
and said to me, 'Go to Siloam and wash'; so I went and washed and
received my sight."

They said to him, "Where is he?"

He said, "I do not know."

They brought to the Pharisees the man who had formerly been blind.
Now it was a sabbath day when Jesus made the clay and opened his eyes.
The Pharisees again asked him how he had received his sight. And he
said to them, "He put clay on my eyes, and I washed, and I see."

Some of the Pharisees said, "This man is not from God, for he does
not keep the sabbath." But others said, "How can a man who is a sinner
do such signs?" There was a division among them.

So they again said to the blind man, "What do you say about him,
since he has opened your eyes?"

He said, "He is a prophet."

The Jews did not believe that he had been blind and had received
his sight, until they called the parents of the man who had received his
sight, and asked them, "Is this your son, who you say was born blind?
How then does he now see?"

His parents answered, "We know that this is our son, and that he
was born blind; but how he now sees we do not know, nor do we know
who opened his eyes. Ask him; he is of age, he will speak for himself."
His parents said this because they feared the Jews, for the Jews had already agreed that if anyone should confess him to be Christ, he was to
be put out of the synagogue. Therefore his parents said, "He is of age,
ask him."

So for the second time they called the man who had been blind, and
said to him, "Give God the praise; we know that this man is a sinner."

He answered, "Whether he is a sinner, I do not know; one thing I
know, that though I was blind, now I see."

They said to him, "What did he do to you? How did he open your
eyes?"

He answered them, "I have told you already, and you would not listen. Why do you want to hear it again? Do you too want to become
his disciples?"

And they reviled him, saying, "You are his disciple, but we are disciples of Moses. We know that God has spoken to Moses, but as for this man, we do not know where he comes from."

The man answered, "Why, this is a marvel! You do not know where he comes from, and yet he opened my eyes. We know that God does not listen to sinners, but if anyone is a worshiper of God and does his will, God listens to him. Never since the world began has it been heard that anyone opened the eyes of a man born blind. If this man were not from God, he could do nothing."

They answered him, "You were born in utter sin, and would you teach us?" And they cast him out.

Jesus heard that they had cast him out, and having found him he said, "Do you believe in the Son of man?"

He answered, "And who is he, sir, that I may believe in him?"

Jesus said to him, "You have seen him, and it is he who speaks to you."

He said, "Lord, I believe"; and he worshiped him.

Jesus said, "For judgment I came into this world, that those who do not see may see, and that those who see may become blind."

Some of the Pharisees near him heard this, and they said to him, "Are we also blind?"

Jesus said to them, "If you were blind, you would have no guilt; but now that you say, 'We see,' your guilt remains."

John 9:1-41

The deacon opens the Book and everything is obliterated by the thickest blackness the Elect have ever known. They blink, and strain to open their eyes, but discover they *are* open. No—this can't be happening! All they had asked for was to see the darkness in themselves (—whatever few, out-of-the-way corners in their hearts that had somehow escaped their notice all these months and so were rather dim—) so they could let the light of Christ into them. But *all* is darkness, in all directions—where are they? How can they get out? Are they alone? Is there anyone who can help them get out? How can they get their bearings? They must be very quiet and listen. If they can maybe hear a sound and figure out what it is and where it's coming from, maybe that will help them know how to get out of this horrifying blackness. They hold their breath and strain their ears and then pick out the voice of the Faithful, sounding strangely far away, calmly going on with their story, saying something about being blind from birth; the Elect hang on every word . . .

The Faithful knew the Elect would not be able to bear the sight of this blackness before today. But in three weeks they will formally renounce their citizenship in the kingdom of darkness, and so they must see the whole truth of life in that kingdom, so they will be able to re-

Luke 9:62

nounce it fully, and, once they have stepped into the kingdom of light, not be tempted to look back. And so the Faithful have exposed the Elect to this harsh light of reality: of themselves, they do not see as God sees—and to not see as God sees is to be blind. The Elect were born blind, in fact, but so were the Faithful, and in the years since Jesus opened their eyes in the waters of illumination, they have learned a great deal about what it means to be born blind, and how Jesus has healed them so they can learn to perceive reality as He does, by His light.

They were born gazing at the world through an obsession for self-aggrandizement; they perceive everything in terms of how it will affect them, what they can get from it. Life is a movie of which they are the star: all others are members of the supporting cast, whose only real significance derives from their relationship to the star, whose roles are important to the extent they enhance the existence of the star in some way; if God is even in the movie, He, too, appears in a supporting role. This is how they were born seeing. But this is not how God sees. No matter what they look at—whether nature or people or even God—they do not see what God sees. When they look upon creation, they see ways they can exploit it; when God looks on creation, He sees it as manifestation of His love and reflection of His glory. When they contemplate the suffering of the innocent, they may see a God who is unjust or nonexistent; when God looks upon unjust suffering, He sees the effects of humanity's turning from Him, and how He has given the life of His Son to bring redemption.

Through the years since their enlightenment in the font, the Faithful have learned that when God looks on all reality, He sees it as it truly is, suffused in the light of His divine compassion; but of themselves, they do not. They have come to see that their congenital blindness so distorts their perception that good can appear as evil. Like the boy in the fairy tale who gets in his eye a splinter from the mirror the devil made to mock God, which magnifies all flaws to conceal the good, making all that is beautiful ugly (which shattered when he fell),—like that child, the Faithful have learned, they perceive reality through the Deceiver's No, and so they do not see things as they really are, as God sees them. They perceive all situations in terms of their own success or failure, approbation or rejection, rather than in terms of God's all-provident love; they are drawn to focus on what displeases them, and to accuse whatever deity they might acknowledge of not looking after their best interests. Seeing everything through the jagged splinter of self-worship, rather than the love of God, they are unable to trust God: "If then the light in you is darkness, how great is the darkness!"

Yet the Faithful stand here today because the giver of all good gifts, the Father of lights, has delivered them from this great darkness in them,

Hans Christian Andersen, *The Snow Queen*

Matt 6:23

Jas 1:17

and given them sight in the healing waters of Baptism. And when this Father adopted them there, He bestowed on them as their inheritance the Spirit He shares with His Son, so that it is now possible for the Faithful to see all things as an obedient son does, in the light of the Father's love. This Spirit would reveal to them ever more deeply all the ways their perception needs to change and give them the means to change it.

And some sense of all this—how the Faithful have come to understand the blindness they were born with and how Jesus gave them sight—is what they are trying to communicate to the Elect by disclosing to them this utter blackness in them at this scrutiny. For in order for the Elect to receive their sight, they must first realize that they truly *are* blind, and ask for help; they must recognize that their natural perception is false, and pray for eyes of faith and trust. Even now they must desire the light Christ gives as deeply as they can, and just as deeply resolve to learn to see by it. For in but three weeks they will be given the capacity to see as God sees; and, so that they will be able to learn to focus their new vision, they must prepare for it by continually reminding themselves that the way that the Lord perceives is the true way; they must approach every situation asking themselves, "How does the Lord look at this? What is His love trying to accomplish here?" They need to practice seeing by faith and desire to grow in it; the God who tells them, "My thoughts are not your thoughts," wants them to understand that His baptismal gift which enables them to be transformed by the renewal of their minds, means that they must allow their thought-life to be transformed, and decide that they will allow the Spirit to teach them a new way of thinking, to give them new thoughts.

The Faithful know from experience how important it is that even before Baptism the Elect are convinced that they need this new way of thinking and determine to learn it, for, after Baptism, in some ways they will be even more vulnerable to the insinuations of their Adversary, who ever plies them with falsehood. Those who have entrusted their lives to a God who is love and take that God seriously, expecting His loving care, will be acutely aware of anything that appears to contradict that love, and the Deceiver will make use of such contradictions to try to undermine their trust. The Faithful have found that when they experience difficulties and reversals, the Deceiver will tempt them to perceive these things as God's unjust rejection, rather than accept them as means through which God can purify their love and so, ultimately, bless them with an even deeper knowledge of His care. As always, the Adversary will seek to turn them against God by trying to persuade them to perceive whatever they are looking at through that jagged splinter of self-worship, that No to God with which he ever seeks

Isa 55:8

to afflict their race: God is not taking care of them, so why should they be concerned for Him? The Faithful have discovered all this from experience and know how crucial it will be for the Elect to refuse to fall back into thinking according to the patterns they learned by perceiving through this all-distorting No, and to learn to perceive instead according to the Spirit of Truth they will receive in Baptism. For the Spirit would free them from the false perception of the Deceiver's deadly lies, and form in them the very mind of Christ, so they can ever grow in knowing the Father as Jesus did, as a Father of infinite compassion— which is their baptismal birthright; they can learn to see all things through Christ's vision of God as loving Father, in trust and gratitude.

John 15:26

1 Cor 2:16

And so because they are veterans of this combat between flesh and spirit that the Elect will soon find themselves plunged into, the Faithful want to prepare their charges for what lies ahead. The Faithful know the Elect cannot comprehend all of this today; it has taken years of learning to see by the light of Christ for these things to become clear to the Faithful. The important thing for the Elect to see today is that, without Christ, they truly are in darkness; whatever they are able to understand of the Faithful's explanation of what this darkness is and how it prevents them from seeing truly, will help them to prepare to learn to use the new vision Christ will give them soon. "Don't be afraid," the Faithful encourage the Elect, "for we saw the blackness you now see, till Jesus touched our eyes; He took away our blindness and we worshipped Him. Listen, it shall be the same for you."

The Elect *are* listening. And as the deacon carefully continues through the long reading, they hear in the story of the man born blind an account of their own progressive illumination: from considering "the man called Jesus," to perceiving Him as a prophet sent by God, to recognizing Him as Redeeming Lord. They understand that the Faithful are being open with them about what baptismal enlightenment will involve them in: bearing witness to those who do not believe, and perhaps bearing the cost of their rejection. As the Elect hear the story unfold, they note how it moves from instance to instance of the contrast between seeing and not seeing, between human perception and God's perception. It is Jesus, not the disciples, who notices the blind man. Perhaps the disciples looked right at him and didn't see him, and when they do look at him they see a problem for academic theological debate: whose sin made him blind? Jesus sees someone suffering and in need of help, through whom God wants to demonstrate His compassion. The Pharisees look at Jesus healing the blind man and see a sinner; the man whose eyes Jesus has opened looks at Him and recognizes Him as Lord. When they contemplate the blind man speaking the truth about what happened to him, the Pharisees see an evil man they must exclude from the worship of God; Jesus sees one He must seek out and draw into even fuller worship of God.

And now the Elect begin to see that in leading them into dense darkness in this Gospel, the Faithful have actually brought them light— that allowing them to see their natural perception as God sees it, allowing them by this terrifying blackness to begin to fathom their utter blindness apart from the light of Christ, is the most brilliant enlightenment the Faithful could have given them today. For as long as the Elect trust in their own self-centered perception and insist they see, they will be blind and can never see; so the Faithful revealed to them their blindness so they would seek to have it healed. "Yes, Lord, we are blind; now we understand. But what now?"

Is the darkness somehow brighter? "I have come as light into the world, that whoever believes in me may not remain in darkness. Desire me as your Light. Be willing to trust me as the Light by which you see, and not your own perception. It is not long before I will anoint your vision. You will see me for who I am and worship me."

John 12:46

Now it is even more clear. To be blind is to perceive through the jagged splinter of the Deceiver's selfish No, to refuse to trust the God of infinite love. To see is (as it was for the man born blind) to see Jesus and worship Him—to recognize in Him the compassionate love of the Father poured out, and know that He is Lord, and thus perceive all things through trust in the divine compassion. And He has promised He will enable them to see: for it is the God who said "Let light shine out of darkness" who will shine in their hearts to give the light of the knowledge of the glory of God in the face of Christ. With Gethsemane's tears He will wash the splinter from their eyes, heal their vision so they can see all by the light of His love.

2 Cor 4:6

As they contemplate this God, who is the only standard of true judgement, who sent Jesus and manifested His very nature in Jesus' healing of the man born blind, the Elect find themselves, as always, between opposite extremes: blindness, and sight; sin, and God's glory revealed; night, and the light of day; sinners whom God does not heed, and worshippers of God who obey Him, to whom He listens; the Pharisees who see from a human perspective and are therefore incapable of true worship, and Jesus, the worshipper of God, who is Himself rightly worshipped.

[Relationship of readings to each other, rite, and faith-experience]

John 8:12

"Jesus said to the Pharisees, 'If you were blind, you would have no guilt; but now that you say, 'We see,' your guilt remains.' " When the Gospel is over, The Elect think back on the readings that preceded it today, and consider them in light of the blackness revealed in them as they stood in the presence of the Light of the World. They had come today with second thoughts about God's loving call to them to be His holy ones, which was enabling them to avoid seeking God to make them holy; they now discern this doubting, not as humility, but as part of the darkness that blinds them, a new disguise for the Deceiver's No. In the first reading, even while the Faithful reaffirmed to them their call, they had also begun to tell the Elect that they needed a change in their perception in order to see reality as God does; the Elect now realize that the psalm the Faithful led them in, in response to that reading, is not only the song of those God has chosen, but also the song of those who *see*, who perceive everything through eyes of trust in God's care, neither taking it for granted nor minimizing it. By filling their minds with the truths which are the reasons why they trust, by picturing for the Elect the true life of God's chosen in the Church under His care, the Faithful were teaching the Elect to begin to perceive as God does. For, the Elect now understand, only to the extent that they allow their minds to be enlightened by the truth of God's care will they be able to avoid stumbling back into the shameful works of darkness that characterized their former way of life; only to the extent that they learn to see all things in light of this new perception, through eyes of trust, will they be able to walk in the new way the epistle exhorts them to, discovering that He who called them to walk these new paths of righteousness is in fact shepherd who will lead them there. He will pour His Spirit on their minds and transform their perception.

As they recall their uncertainties when they arrived today, the Elect reflect that if the Faithful had simply told them they were blind, they could not have borne it. Because the Faithful first assured them that they were God's chosen, whose every need He will provide, they could know that He would give them the healing from blindness He has now given them such a longing for. Only when the Elect were secure in God's choosing of them did the Faithful speak to them of the splinter that distorts their vision, reveal to them the full horror of their blindness; and even then, the Faithful proceeded gradually: pointing out to them in the Old Testament lesson that God does not see as humankind; then, in the epistle, that they must wake and ask Christ for light; and, not until the Gospel, that the fact is that the change in perception they need is so radical that they are blind without it.

The readings have worked together to help the Elect understand what they are asking for in the waters of enlightenment; only if the Elect comprehend what God is promising will they be able to prepare for it so they can receive it in fullness. The psalm reminds them of the sacramental dimension of full membership in the Church where they will dwell forever; the reflections of one who was chosen by God, anointed, and given the Spirit, provide the Elect with a meditation on what it will mean for them to be anointed with the Spirit who will always be with them, even in the shadow of death—a meditation that will inform and enrich their experience when they *are* anointed, and receive their sight, and are able to walk as children of light. Similarly, the psalm assures them that even if now they find themselves confronted by the presence of their ancient foe, God is preparing a feast for them all the while.

Through the readings, as through the intercessions and exorcism to follow, the Spirit works to accomplish the purpose of the scrutiny: "to complete the conversion of the Elect and deepen their resolve to RCIA 141 hold fast to Christ and to carry out their decision to love God above all." At the Rite of Election the Faithful made it clear that the baptized life is a life of wanting what God wants; at this Second Scrutiny, they explain that in order to want what God wants, the Elect must see as God sees. This scrutiny uncovers for the Elect the reality that the darkness in their lives is not only sinful actions, but also the false perception that leads to those actions; to avoid doing the works of darkness they must seek to be healed of their darkened perception. Yet the readings have revealed not only a deeper level of weakness and sin which the Elect can now bring to the community's intercession and exorcism for healing, but also the good that God is working in them: their continuing willingness to listen to God's Word and accept it as criterion by which their lives are understood. As last Sunday the Elect found themselves thirsting to know Christ as Living Water, true source of their existence, now they discover they desire to know Him even more intimately, as Light, as illuminating love through which they perceive all things, by whose radiance they perform all their actions; they understand in a deeper way how much they need baptismal enlightenment, and therefore they long for it even more.

Unaccustomed to their new-found blindness, the Elect are glad when their godparents lead them forward for the community's intercession. RCIA 166 "Elect of God, kneel down and pray."

Each of the Elect has seen through the scrutiny specific ways in which darkness still rules his or her life, in actions as well as the ways of perceiving that inform those actions, and each of the Faithful know from experience particular ways in which blindness has afflicted them; in the time of silent intercession, each prays by the light he or she has been given . . . May the Elect be willing to have their perception changed, and come to see as God sees: May they see God as Light-Giver, Compassionate Healer . . . May they (like Jesus) see those in need as those they are called to help; may they see all people they encounter as the beloved for whom Christ died . . . May they see themEph 1:4 selves as God's chosen, that they should be holy and blameless before Him, whenever they are tempted not to trust . . . May they see evil and human sin, not as opportunities for accusing God, but as His beckoning them to lay down their lives in forgiveness and selfless service . . .

And as the Faithful intercede for the Elect according to the Spirit's prompting, the Elect themselves bring the blindness in thought and actions they have today seen in their lives, to the Voice they heard speak of the works of God being made manifest: Lord, give us sight, they pray.

RCIA 167   The Faithful help the Elect to their feet, for all must stand for the Church's solemn prayer . . . May the Elect truly know Christ as Light, and whatever they look at, see it by that Light, so they may desire what God desires, value what God values, and pursue it . . . And when the Faithful have prayed in the petitions of the rite that the Elect, roused from the darkness of their deadly sleep, may be given perseverance in their resolve to walk in the light, they add similar intercessions for themselves; they conclude with prayer that the Word proclaimed at this scrutiny will bear the fruit of light in all the world.

RCIA 168   Then, to seal their intercession, the Faithful add the word of deliverance that they are empowered to give. "Father of mercy . . ." hear the Elect, and they pray, "We want to see you as merciful Father; help us to know you that way." ". . . Free these Elect . . ." "Yes, free us," they pray, "from unbelief, from the doubt of darkened minds, from

John 8:44   all the false values with which the Father of Lies is blinding us; set us free from any ways he has distorted our vision through the splinter of his No, which prevents us from receiving and giving the love of God. Ground our minds in trust in Christ who is the Truth, so we will be able to walk as children of light." "Lord Jesus . . ." "To see by any other light than you is to be blind. Shine in our hearts your gladdening

Phos hilaron   light that dispels all darkness, so that someday we may see you face to face." ". . . for you are Lord forever and ever." "Yes we will trust you to be our Light." "Amen." Their useless vision feels a healing pressure. "Go, set out for Siloam. In three weeks' time I will meet you at the waters, and when you have washed you will see all things made new."

The rite has exposed their blindness to scrutiny, enabled the Elect to see it, and stirred up in them the desire to be rid of it so that they seek to be healed, for only if they truly desire to be healed of their blindness will they be able to be. As they prepare for the final blessing, those once darkness, who soon will be light in the Lord, recall once more that they are in a land of promises and warnings. Three of the readings have spoken of anointing; the Elect have been assured that they *are* chosen, and promised that only three weeks hence they will be anointed with a deeper knowledge that God has chosen them than they can even imagine now. But the Elect have also been warned: being God's chosen may not always mean what they expect, for they are blind; for to see is not to see according to human perception, but to see as Jesus sees, and they can only see this way if He opens their eyes and gives Himself to them as Light.

But today they are still journeying through the shadowlands, and RCIA 169 it is time to set out on the next stage of their journey. "Dear Elect, go in peace, and join us again at the next scrutiny. May the Lord remain with you always."

"Amen"; and they turn to feel their way toward the sound of the Voice that offered Himself to them as Light. They came seeing through the self-worship of their No, and so they came blind; they leave perceiving how blind they are, and so now they begin to see.

VI. The Third Scrutiny

"In order to inspire in the elect a desire for purification and redemption by Christ, three scrutinies are celebrated. By this means, first of all, the elect are instructed gradually about the mystery of sin, from which the whole world and every person longs to be delivered and thus saved from its present and future consequences. . . . From the first to the final scrutiny the elect should progress in their perception of sin and their desire for salvation" (no. 143).

RCIA

nos. 7, 9, 20, 30,
138–146, 171–177

Lectionary, Fifth Sunday of Lent, A

Ezek 37:12-14
Ps 130:1-2, 3-4, 5-7a, 7bc-8
Rom 8:8-11
John 11:1-45

Dead. Dead, that is how they are. They feel like they will never move again. And numb. They are so numb they ache with numbness. They never could have imagined it would be like this. So long ago, it seems another lifetime, so long ago they had heard they were dead in their sins, they needed to put that death to death, and it sounded so romantic. Only two weeks away now; it is not romantic at all. They are dead, just dead; they cannot move. And where is God—the God who brings water bursting from rocks, and enkindles faith in hearts, and gives sight to the blind? No, that God is not here in this nothingness, this No Place where they find themselves, if He is anywhere, if He even exists . . .

Five weeks ago, when the Elect were so full of hope (or was it just nervous energy?), they willingly followed the Faithful into this Lenten desert to be tested, to allow the full dimensions of their No to be exposed by the Sun of Righteousness, and consumed by the blazing of His jealous love, and healed in the wings of His passionate Yes. And when, in the clear air of this dry solitude, His fiery rays revealed to them the ways that they did not trust Him—say Yes to Him—as provident source of everything that comes to them, they brought their No to Him, asked Him to purify them, to give them the grace to accept Him as Living Water. And then when His relentless radiance illumined for them all the ways they did not trust Him—say Yes to Him—as means of their perception, again they brought their No to Him (though it was harder this time), and asked Him to refine them, to give them the grace to know Him as their Light. But today by His Love's fierce brightness they behold themselves in this desolate, dried-out valley, which is the last stronghold of their No, and they see no way they can get out.

Mal 4:2

The Elect know that what God asks of them in Baptism is a complete Yes, at whatever level each of them is capable of saying it, and for many months now (and especially these last weeks of purification and enlightenment) they have sought to surrender to God's articulation of that Yes within them. Now there is only one significant way left that they are resisting that Yes, but it is the hardest No to let go of, the one they have held onto, protected, the longest, because they know they can't survive without it. But because it separates them from God it is sin, and because it is sin it brings them death and they must give it up, and in the steady brilliance of the Sun of Righteousness they cannot fail to see this stark reality.

The Elect are young adults, middle-aged, elderly; they come from all classes of society; each approaches Baptism shaped by a life journey different from that of the others. The stubborn No that confronts them today may well take a different form for each, but for each it is whatever aspect of their death in sin that they still cling to, which

God would enable them to bring to Him, so that He can free them from its power to destroy them. For some it may be a particular sin, or pattern of sin, to which they have been attached for so long they never allowed themselves to perceive it as sin, perhaps until they submitted themselves to seeing by Christ as their perception; now they can see it as sin, but they can't see how they can ever separate themselves from it. Perhaps the No some of the Elect find themselves confronting today is a long-buried refusal to forgive someone whose grave injustice against them brought them great loss and lasting suffering, a suffering perhaps intensified by the fact that the one who inflicted it has the reputation of being a "good Christian."

For others who are older, the final No separating them from God—the last remaining serious way they have hardened their hearts against Him—may be some carefully repressed refusal to trust Him in an encounter with senseless evil that left them in agonizing pain. Perhaps the one they most loved and trusted betrayed them. Perhaps they or someone they knew who devoted all their energy and time to helping those in desperate need, was stricken with a wasting or crippling illness that brought an end to their life-giving work. Or perhaps (in a culture where death is the only remaining obscenity—where most people have never been with a person who is dying or seen a corpse) they have experienced the horrible or untimely death of someone they loved, maybe even a child killed in a needless accident. Most people do not pass through life unscathed by the Problem of Evil; it may even have been what prompted the Elect to begin seeking God in the first place.

And now, when the journey the Elect began in the catechumenate has brought them so close to the springs of salvation, it may well be that their refusal to trust God in an encounter with the Problem of Evil is the last refuge of their selfish No; yet anyone who would honestly make the baptismal profession of faith in a God of infinite love and infinite power, who has lived through times when God allowed what God could not allow and still be God (still be all-loving and all-powerful), must be willing to say Yes to God even when God seems not to be God, even in the Problem of Evil. The Elect understand this, yet they do not experience their No as refusal, but as inability, as paralysis; somehow they can't move, can't go any further. Now as never before they are experiencing how utterly dead they are in their No—in their sin—on their own. Here, in this parched No Place, they contemplate the remains of their once-vibrant aspirations to holiness, strewn like bleached bones of desert wayfarers who never made it home, in heaps throughout this valley, the last bastion of their No. Wretched ones that we are, who will deliver us from this No which is our death?

Isa 12:3

Rom 7:24

The Faithful have read their thoughts. "Behold, you say, you are dried up, your hope is lost, you are clean cut off. Therefore, God gives us this Word for you":

> Thus says the Lord God: Behold, I will open your graves, and raise you from your graves, O my people; and I will bring you home into the land of Israel. And you shall know that I am the Lord, when I open your graves, and raise you from your graves, O my people. And I will put my Spirit within you, and you shall live, and I will place you in your own land; then you shall know that I, the Lord, have spoken, and I have done it, says the Lord.

So now these dead, lying far from home, are addressed by One who is known as Lord because He brings life even from death, who is Homebringer, whose Word, promising to give life, *gives* life, does what it says. With this Word of command and power, He promises the Elect that He will deliver them from even the ultimate outworking of their sinful No, which is death; that He will breathe His Spirit into them so they can live; that He will bring them to their true homeland; and that they will *know* Him as God by experiencing that this Word of His saying what He will do for them is true. With Ezekiel, the Faithful prophesy this Word, because they have already experienced that God has spoken and acted, that He does what He promises: He has opened the graves where they were buried in the isolation of their sin, raised them from this death, given them a homeland where they live by His Spirit; yet the Faithful also know that, in another sense, they are still in exile, and so with this Word they remind themselves that they, too, look forward to a further fulfillment of God's promise.

Through this Word, the Faithful have provided for the Elect images to clothe their ossified hopes with flesh. But merely being present on an occasion when the Word of Promise is proclaimed may not be enough for those yet dead in sin, if they do not understand how to respond to it. As the Faithful help the Elect prepare to say the deepest Yes of which they are capable at this point in their lives, they must help them to understand how their No is yet working to prevent them from giving themselves to God: how they cooperate with their death in sin, how the Deceiver continually infiltrates their thoughts to tempt them to keep repeating His No; in order to be able to respond to God's Word with their Yes, so that He can raise them from the death of their No, the Elect must be aware of the nature of the temptations assaulting them, so that they can resist them. Whatever form taken by the deadly No the Elect struggle with (a pattern of sin they find themselves powerless against, an inability to forgive someone, an incapacity for

trusting God in whatever manifestation of the Problem of Evil has touched their lives), and whatever temptation the Deceiver may em-
1 Cor 10:13
ploy to keep them buried in that No, the Faithful have already encountered it, and can help the Elect to recognize it for the lie it is, and warn them not to be deceived into remaining in their No.

"If a loving God allows this, who cares if God is loving, for God's love is meaningless," the Deceiver may prompt them, seeking to lure them toward either the extreme of overindulgent anger at God that will cut them off from their only source of healing, or the opposite extreme of repression of their anger, and resignation to a God who is, quite simply, horrible. Perhaps he will then tempt them, as when they are hurt in human relationships, to withdraw to where it is safe, to polite interactions where they no longer fully share themselves, where expectations are so lowered there is no longer possibility of hurt. Perhaps he will nudge them toward the quicksand of self-pity, to suck them once more into the self-worship of their No. Surrendering to any of these temptations will make the Elect incapable of receiving the life that is being offered them, but no matter what temptation may assail them, the Faithful have struggled with it and more, and can share with the Elect how they have learned to triumph over it.

As the Elect survey the eerie valley where they lie lifeless in the sin which is their exile, they see they are surrounded by opposite extremes: those buried in graves, and those who have been raised; those in exile, and those at home in their own land; those dead, without Spirit, and those living because of the Spirit; those not knowing the Lord, and those who truly know Israel's Lord is God. "And I will put my Spirit within you and you shall live, and I will place you in your own land; then you shall know that I, the Lord, have spoken, and I have done it, says the Lord."

But still they cannot move. "We have listened to your Word, but we don't feel any different. You say God can do something, but how can such as we believe it? We cannot let go of this last No which comes between us and Him; we see it is our death, because it is sin, but we cannot let it go. Where is this God who claims to raise the dead? Last week you said He would be with us even in the valley overshadowed by death, but here there is no sign of Him: in this valley all we see are the remains of our desire to know a loving God; all we see in this valley are our dried-up hopes. What will ever make it different?" they sigh.

The Faithful know that faith grows in the heart as it is proclaimed out loud; with patience born of the fact that they have seen this valley before, and asked the same question themselves, the Faithful motion the Elect to sing with them.

Ps 130:7bc   ℞ With the Lord there is mercy, and fullness of redemption.

Out of the depths I cry to thee, O Lord!
  Lord, hear my voice!
Let thy ears be attentive
  to the voice of my supplications!

If thou, O Lord, shouldst mark iniquities,
  Lord, who could stand?
But there is forgiveness with thee,
  that thou mayest be feared.

I wait for the Lord, my soul waits,
  and in his word I hope;
my soul waits for the Lord
  more than watchmen for the morning,
  more than watchmen for the morning.
O Israel, hope in the Lord!

For with the Lord there is steadfast love,
  and with him is plenteous redemption.
And he will redeem Israel
  from all his iniquities.

Ps 130:1-2,
3-4, 5-7a,
7bc-8

As the Elect hear the opening verses of the psalm, they realize that the cantor is giving voice to what is in their hearts, as they cry to the Lord from the depths of this bleak valley, suppliants begging to be heard. They recognize themselves, unable to move in the pitch-blackness of their iniquity, waiting for the Lord with greater longing than watchmen for daybreak.

But the Faithful are singing this, too, repeating the refrain and praying in silent agreement as the psalmist proclaims the verses. As the Elect hear them begging for mercy, they wonder why the Faithful would pray such a prayer; if they had thought conversion was over at Baptism, now it is clear that is not so. The Faithful have not attained some comfortable plateau of "goodness"; centuries of seeking God have taught them that an ever-deepening union with a God of infinite love in this life requires an ever-deeper discovery of the ways they thoughtlessly exclude Him from their lives, repenting of these things and turning from them. This is why the Faithful, generation after generation, keep returning to the Lenten wilderness, to seek out and confront the ways in which they are unfaithful, and cry to God for mercy and healing on the basis of their experience that He gives it. They share their journey to the purifying wilderness with the Elect to show them that their God, before whom none crushed under the weight of sin can stand, is merciful, offers plenteous redemption, bearing the full cost of releasing them from sin's burden; He loves steadfastly, and offers abounding forgiveness, and so they honor Him with awe. With Israel, the Faithful call themselves and the Elect to hope in the Lord on the basis of what they have seen Him do, knowing that He will redeem; all the Elect must do is repent of as much of their No as they are able to be aware of now, bring it to the font, and leave it there.

And the Elect can begin now, in praying the psalm: from the depths of whatever situation they find themselves in which is separating them from God, from the depths of their inability to find Him there, they can cry out, for this makes it possible for them to be heard and delivered. And even as they cry out, the Elect must also proclaim what is true, even when they don't see it—which they do by joining in the psalm refrain; as they sing it, now and in the week to come, they will remind themselves of the truth that God hears them, that He offers redemption to the full for the sin which makes them dead, and their trust will deepen.

And now in their deadness, while they are still trying to understand how they can be separated from the No which is their death, the Elect must simply wait, as those of lesser importance wait for those of greater importance, acknowledging their dependence; the Faithful exhort them to wait *in hope*, in the trust that God's Word is true, that although they can't see it in their depths, there is a steadfast love so powerful it will bring life even when life isn't possible. As they wait, they find themselves, as always, between opposite extremes: iniquity deserving punishment, and forgiveness and redemption; the night of waiting, and the dawn.

"With the Lord there is mercy, and fullness of redemption." The Elect had asked how such as they could ever believe God could raise them from the paralyzing No that leaves them lifeless, and the Faithful have begun to answer this by leading the Elect to join them in proclaiming the truth of God's redemptive love and waiting for it. But what if, by some miracle they can't imagine, they get free of this last specific deadly No and speak Baptism's Yes? How can they ever live it out? The No in them they once thought they could erase with a reasonable amount of well-meaning effort, they have now discovered motivates them much more totally than they ever could have thought possible, and they are utterly powerless against it. Even if they are delivered from the particular articulation of this No oppressing them today, and proclaim their Yes in the font, how is it possible that they will not soon enough find themselves articulating it in a new way, and fall back into living in the No that repels them from God? "We will hope in your Word, in your power to redeem us, but how can it be that we can live a *life* that is redeemed?" The lector turns the page.

Those who are in the flesh cannot please God.

But you are not in the flesh, you are in the Spirit, if the Spirit of God really dwells in you. Anyone who does not have the Spirit of Christ does not belong to him. But if Christ is in you, although your bodies are dead because of sin, your spirits are alive because of righteousness. If the Spirit of him who raised Jesus from the dead dwells in you, he who raised Christ Jesus from the dead will give life to your mortal bodies also through his Spirit who dwells in you.

Rom 8:8-11

Even as they did last Sunday, the Faithful provide the Elect with the knowledge they need by sharing with them God's Word to those already baptized this Fifth Sunday of Lent. As the Faithful reflect on how it is that God has delivered them from the spiritual death of sin and the physical death it brings with it, and how He enables them to persevere in the new existence He has given them, they reassure the Elect that it is indeed possible to live the risen life.

True, of themselves, the Faithful are "in the flesh," bound up in the selfishness that prevents them from speaking the Yes which is pleasing to God, and so they are subject to death. But when they gave themselves to God in Baptism, He fulfilled the promise they just heard Him give Ezekiel and gave them His own Spirit, and as that Spirit enabled them to allow Him to make His home in them, they found Him releasing them from the constraints of self-worship. For this Spirit of the awe-full God of the first lesson is also the Spirit of His obedient Son who thus animates them with His righteousness, making them pleasing to God: although the bodies they have now remain mortal, who they truly are will live forever. If this Spirit of the almighty God who raised His Son is living in them, then this same God will raise their bodies even as He raised Christ's, by the power of this Spirit—His Spirit—living in them.

Through this reading the Faithful seek to impress upon the Elect the magnitude of the gift God will give them at Baptism when He sends His own Spirit to indwell them. Those seeking Baptism cannot say they want to be Christians—to belong to Christ—and ignore His Spirit, for it is Christ's indwelling Spirit who makes them belong to Him: unless Christ's Spirit lives in them, they cannot belong to Him. As long as they cling to their selfish nature that ever says No to God, they simply cannot please Him; but if by grace they will allow the Spirit to replace this selfish nature as the center of their existence—if they will learn to live by Christ's Spirit, not "in the flesh"—they will be able to live the Yes that pleases God. This baptismal gift of the Spirit of God is not a metaphor that some can find meaningful; it is not an abstract theory. It is the life-changing reality that Paul met with in Baptism, and the Faithful speak these words with him because they know exactly what he is talking about and are themselves seeking to live it.

Acts 9:17-18

But as much as the Faithful emphasize the reality and power of God's gift of His Spirit, they also seek to ensure that the Elect don't misunderstand and think that, once they have received the Spirit, their selfish nature (their "flesh") will cease to exist. The Faithful must make it clear, especially when the Elect are locked in mortal combat with their No, that even in the baptized the flesh is yet at war with the Spirit. The Spirit *will* enable the Elect to speak the Yes of Baptism, and, once He establishes His center of command in them, bring them to final victory over their selfish nature; but the Elect will not be passive spectators: in the power of His grace, and armed with His wisdom, they must willingly do battle with the flesh.

The Faithful have discovered that the principal battleground in this war between flesh and Spirit is their minds, and its outcome depends in large measure on whether the thoughts deployed there are loyal to God or to their selfish nature. Since it is thus crucial for them to know the allegiance of their thoughts, the Faithful have learned to ask the Spirit to make them aware of the unconscious assumptions that underlie the thoughts they entertain, and they explain this to the Elect—for whatever arguments their flesh is assaulting them with to persuade them they cannot pronounce Baptism's Yes, may well assail them after they have spoken that Yes to prevent them from experiencing its life-giving power. The Elect will discover that whatever No may yet separate them from giving themselves to God—a pattern of sin, an inability to forgive, or to trust—what underlies it is the desire to hold onto their own way of evaluating and responding to things, a Job-like plaint that God's way isn't fair; whatever form their selfish No may take for each, at its root is the demand that God has to be God on *their* terms—that they, not God, should be God.

Rom 8:5-6   If they continually entertain such thoughts, setting their minds on the demands of their flesh to be their god, they will find the way they

Gal 5:19-21   live dictated by the flesh—by idolatry, anger, impurity, and the like—in

Rom 8:7   hostility to God that brings death. If they allow the Spirit to direct their

Phil 4:8   thoughts, filling them with what is true and gracious and worthy of

Gal 5:22-23   praise, they will find their lives bearing the fruit of love, joy, and long-

Rom 8:5b-6   suffering, which will bring life and peace. Yet even as the Faithful explain to the Elect that what will enable them to live no longer "in the flesh" but in the Spirit, is to set their minds on the things of the Spirit, they reassure them that doing this is not up to their own desperate men-

2 Cor 10:5   tal exertion. Their thoughts will become captive to Christ, as Christ's Spirit inspires in them Christ's thoughts, and they grace-fully welcome them to replace the selfish schemings of their flesh.

The Elect had asked how it could be possible for them to live out the Yes they would give to God—God would give them to give—in

only two weeks time; as the epistle comes to an end they consider what they have heard. More clearly than ever, they see that what they have been preparing for all these months is the gift of God's Spirit: when His Spirit dwells in them He will free them from living by the dictates of their selfish No, so they will be able to please God. When Christ by His Spirit lives in them, His righteousness will make who they are alive, even though the bodies they have now will die; and God who by His Spirit raised His anointed Son, will by that Spirit living in the Elect ultimately give life to their sin-condemned bodies as well. As always, their progress to salvation is lived out between opposite extremes: in the flesh and not pleasing to God, and in the Spirit; not belonging to Christ, and having Christ's Spirit that makes them belong to Him; bodies rendered mortal because of sin, and spirits alive because of righteousness; mortality, and being raised to life by the Spirit. "If the Spirit of Him who raised Jesus from the dead dwells in you, He who raised Christ Jesus from the dead will give life to your mortal bodies also through His Spirit who dwells in you."

When the liturgy began today, the Elect found themselves gazing on the desiccation of their dreams of loving God, wondering how things could ever be different for any so dead in their sin as they. The Faithful told them that God by His Spirit would raise them, encouraged them to believe His Word of redemption and cry out to Him, which is the first step toward being raised, and explained how Christ's indwelling Spirit animates them with His righteousness so they can live a life that is redeemed. But what of the specific articulation of their No that keeps them yet lying in death's dark bonds, and the specific temptations to it they find themselves wrapped up in?

"You have told us to hope in the Word that God speaks, in His promise to raise our death to life; you have explained how He brings this life about. But still we are entombed in the separation of our No. We understand what you have said, but we need more than explanations; to be able to believe merciful redemption is possible even for us, even in these depths, we need a flesh-and-blood example. Show us what it is like when He raises people from their deepest depths of No—you told us *how*, now show us *that* He gives the Spirit's Yes that brings life forever."

John 11:25a, 26

℣ I am the resurrection and the life, said the Lord:
he who believes in me will not die forever.

A certain man was ill, Lazarus of Bethany, the village of Mary and her sister Martha. It was Mary who anointed the Lord with ointment and wiped his feet with her hair, whose brother Lazarus was ill. So the sisters sent to him, saying, "Lord, he whom you love is ill."

But when Jesus heard it he said, "This illness is not unto death, it is for the glory of God, so that the Son of God may be glorified by means of it."

Now Jesus loved Martha and her sister and Lazarus. So when he heard that he was ill, he stayed two days longer in the place where he was. Then after this he said to the disciples, "Let us go into Judea again."

The disciples said to him, "Rabbi, the Jews were but now seeking to stone you, and are you going there again?"

Jesus answered, "Are there not twelve hours in the day? If anyone walks in the day, he does not stumble, because he sees the light of this world. But if anyone walks in the night, he stumbles, because the light is not in him." Thus he spoke, and then he said to them, "Our friend Lazarus has fallen asleep, but I go to awake him out of sleep."

The disciples said to him, "Lord, if he has fallen asleep, he will recover."

Now Jesus had spoken of his death, but they thought that he meant taking rest in sleep. Then Jesus told them plainly, "Lazarus is dead; and for your sake I am glad that I was not there, so that you may believe. But let us go to him."

Thomas, called the Twin, said to his fellow disciples, "Let us also go, that we may die with him."

Now when Jesus came, he found that Lazarus had already been in the tomb four days. Bethany was near Jerusalem, about two miles off, and many of the Jews had come to Martha and Mary to console them concerning their brother. When Martha heard that Jesus was coming she went and met him, while Mary sat in the house. Martha said to Jesus, "Lord, if you had been here, my brother would not have died. And even now I know that whatever you ask from God, God will give you."

Jesus said to her, "Your brother will rise again."

Martha said to him, "I know that he will rise again in the resurrection at the last day."

Jesus said to her, "I am the resurrection and the life; he who believes in me, though he die, yet shall he live, and whoever lives and believes in me shall never die. Do you believe this?"

She said to him, "Yes, Lord; I believe that you are the Christ, the Son of God, he who is coming into the world."

When she had said this, she went and called her sister Mary, saying quietly, "The Teacher is here and is calling for you." And when she heard it, she rose quickly and went to him. Now Jesus had not yet come to the village but was still in the place where Martha had met him. When the Jews who were with her in the house, consoling her, saw Mary rise quickly and go out, they followed her, supposing that she was going to the tomb to weep there.

Then Mary, when she came where Jesus was and saw him, fell at his feet, saying to him, "Lord, if you had been here, my brother would not have died."

When Jesus saw her weeping, and the Jews who came with her also weeping, he was deeply moved in spirit and troubled; and he said, "Where have you laid him?"

They said to him, "Lord, come and see."

Jesus wept. So the Jews said, "See how he loved him!" But some of them said, "Could not he who opened the eyes of the blind man have kept this man from dying?"

Then Jesus, deeply moved again, came to the tomb; it was a cave, and a stone lay upon it. Jesus said, "Take away the stone."

Martha, the sister of the dead man, said to him, "Lord, by this time there will be an odor, for he has been dead four days."

Jesus said to her, "Did I not tell you that if you would believe you would see the glory of God?"

So they took away the stone. And Jesus lifted up his eyes and said, "Father, I thank thee that thou hast heard me. I knew that thou hearest me always, but I have said this on account of the people standing by, that they may believe that thou didst send me." When he had said this, he cried with a loud voice, "Lazarus, come out!"

The dead man came out, his hands and feet bound with bandages, and his face wrapped with a cloth. Jesus said to them, "Unbind him, and let him go."

Many of the Jews therefore, who had come with Mary and had seen what he did, believed in him.

John 11:1-45

In the acclamation, the cantor sings of resurrection, but the Elect still feel as they did at the beginning of the liturgy. One final way of saying No to God yet comes between them and God and thus keeps them dead in their sin; they cannot raise themselves to life and they cannot even *be* raised unless they are willing to be raised, to die to their sin which is death, and so the Faithful must help them learn to be willing by showing them that it is possible: telling how it happened to them. If the No that restrains the Elect is a besetting sin that they can't imagine themselves without, the Faithful can help them by repeating on a deeper level what they had already explained in aiding them to turn from other sins during the catechumenate; if the Elect are bound up in a deadly lack of forgiveness, the Faithful can help them find freedom by beginning to speak of some of the Word they will proclaim in greater depth at the Presentation of the Lord's Prayer, in but a few days' time.

And if the No that holds the Elect prisoner to death in sin is a refusal to trust in the face of the Problem of Evil, the Faithful can minister to them by sharing what they themselves have learned. Some of the Elect may not yet have encountered the pain of this No; others may have repressed it, to find it only now drawn to the surface of their con-

RCIA 141

sciousness by the light of the scrutinies. But whether the Elect have yet encountered it or not, at some point the Faithful must be honest with them about the Problem of Evil: God's love for the Elect does not mean that they are baptized into a life of living happily ever after, but into a life of faith (which is what they asked for in the very first rite of the catechumenate); evil things occur in life which to even the most just believer are utterly unjust, and the baptized are not automatically exempt from them. And if some of the Elect are now tightly wound up in such an agony that leaves them unable to trust a loving God, the Faithful tell the story of how they themselves were freed to trust.

"We know your pain that no one understands, for we have borne it too. There was a time when, paralyzed by that pain, we could not move, we could not trust; we saw not trusting separated us from God, but we were dead in our desire to determine what things mean, we could not move ourselves to trust. Like you, we found ourselves bounced back and forth between two antipodes: anger at a God who was Tormentor, and agonized acceptance of a cruel God—which alienated us from Him as much as anger; we simply couldn't find a middle place between them. But then on Calvary we stumbled on the philosopher's stone, and finally found the place of rest we sought; for there we saw earth's one true alchemist, from His strange workshop on the Cross, change evil's lead to gold. There we learned to allow God to give us faith that when He permits what seems most unloving and destructive, He will redeem it to be radiant with His love; we learned as Joseph did to entrust to God what had been meant for evil, so He could work it for good."

1 Cor 1:23
1 Pet 2:4-8

Gen 50:20
Rom 8:28

The Faithful explain what they have experienced, that the only way out of the anguish of unjust suffering is to allow it to be redeemed by the Cross, which transformed even the worst evil—sin—to salvation; the first step toward allowing one's suffering to be redemptive is to accept God as knowing what is best for the salvation of all He has created. What life is about, what the Elect have been brought into existence for, is to become ever more Christ-like, more faithful, so they can receive the capacity on ever deeper levels to love and praise forever in heaven; everything God allows to happen is intended to work toward this end. "Rejoice always" is a hard word, but what it calls for is that Christians care more about God's desire to shape them in the image of His Son, and about believing that He is working in their lives to accomplish this, than about anything else.

Phil 4:4

However, the Faithful warn the Elect, they have also learned that the same circumstances God wants to use for their transformation in holiness, their Adversary would use to destroy them. Ways in which they encounter the Problem of Evil in their lives can bring the Elect

closer to God or separate them from Him, depending on how they perceive them, so the Deceiver bombards them with the thought that there
is no way the evil that afflicts them can be consistent with a loving
God. The willingness to trust God in their perception, which the Elect
have already begun to pray for, grows to true maturity in the struggle
with the Problem of Evil. Those who survive its crushing grip have
learned that faith is three-dimensional perception: when two lines cut
across each other on the flat page of a book, they appear to touch each
other, but if the lines could be seen in three dimensions, it is quite possible they do not intersect; in the plane of human experience, unjust
evil seems necessarily to imply a God who is not loving, but the depth
dimension of faith reveals a gap between the premise and the conclusion.

And the Elect can learn this three-dimensional perception of faith—
Heb 12:2   the obedience of faith—from the pioneer in obedience, who, Son though
Heb 5:8   He was, learned obedience through suffering; if they are to perceive
their situation as God does, they must see it through Christ's eyes, for
His trusting love of the Father who is perfect Love, in which He died,
is stronger even than the Problem of Evil. As the Elect allow His Spirit
to give them the breath to speak with Him His Yes of total love and
trust which He spoke from the Cross, and to sustain it, they will find
themselves raised from the death of their No to a God who seemed
the opposite of love; in the Cross they will discover the true
philosopher's stone, transforming the basest of evil into shining
redemption.

. . . As the Elect listen to the words of the Faithful, who last week
told them of a man who was born blind so God's loving work could
be manifest through him, and now of a man whose death was so God
could be glorified, they cannot help but notice that the story of Lazarus itself is an illustration of how God can turn evil to good. But whether
the death of the No still binding the Elect is a refusal to trust in affliction by the Problem of Evil, or some other sin, the Gospel makes it
clear that God in Christ is committed to raising them from it.

In this Gospel the Elect see how the God who made and orders all
has revealed who He is in the compassion of His Son Jesus, whom He
always hears. In Martha and Mary, the Elect see the Faithful, who know
Jesus as *the* Teacher, who believe He is the one the Father has anointed
and know the Father will give Him what He asks—so the Faithful have
sent for their friend Jesus to come and help the Elect. And as they lie
yet lifeless in the tomb with Lazarus, the Elect hear themselves described,
over and over, as the ones this Lord loves; when they cannot move
to come to Him, He has come to them where they are wrapped up in
their insistence on being their own gods, sealed up in the dark cave
of their refusal to trust His love, utterly without life, to raise them.

His deep care for them so moves Him that He is angry at what the death which is sin has done to them, and He weeps over their corruption. And they lie motionless, rotting in their No: " 'Our soul is waiting for the Lord, we count on His Word . . .' "

Ps 130:5

Gen 1

"Know that my Word is near. As at Creation each thing was named and so came into being, so shall it be for you. When in the waters you are buried with me, plunged into my Passion, you will hear me summon you to life. 'I baptize you,' you will hear my servant say; then in a loud voice I shall cry out your name. 'Come out!' I will command, and my Word will raise you from your death in sin and give you life. Desire me—only me—as your Life. Desire my love for the Father as your Life, and not the putrefaction of your No. For I myself am Resurrection, and when you are united with me in the font, I myself will share with you my life."

Rom 6:3-11
RCIA 226
John 11:43

As the Elect imagine the scene of their resurrection, they cannot help but notice how Jesus brings it about, as He did Lazarus', in the midst of a community. It is by the prayers of those who love them, the Faithful, and in their presence, that the Elect will be raised. It is the Faithful who take away the stone, removing any obstacle to the Elect's Yes by their teaching, who, once the Elect are raised, work to free them from the graveclothes of whatever habitual assumptions may yet cling to them that could hinder them from walking freely in their new existence. And then perhaps others who see the change in them from sin's death to life will come to believe in the One who gave that life. But the scene is yet two weeks away, and in the meantime, the Elect will continue to find their way to it marked by pairs of opposites: being bound, and being unbound; unbelief, and faith; death, and resurrection.

"Many of the Jews, therefore, who had come with Mary and had seen what He did, believed in Him." In the silence after the Gospel the Elect consider the distance over which the Faithful through their Word have carried them this day. In all their long journey from the land of unlikeness, the Valley of Dry Bones was the strangest and most forbidding place they had seen, where they found themselves haunted by their now-skeletal hopes of a holy life. But in this macabre valley the Faithful proclaimed to them not only that God promised them His Spirit, and life and a home in His kingdom, but that they will know that it was truly He who had spoken, and that He is God, when they experience Him fulfilling His Word in their lives: giving them His Spirit stirring in them, and a new life, and a home under His reign. Then, in the psalm, the Faithful led the Elect in the prayer of dead Israel to be revived from sin's death, which the epistle reminded them could only be accomplished by the Spirit, who alone gives life; for God's Spirit

[Relationship of readings to each other, rite, and faith-experience]

who raises the bones of Israel, is also Christ's Spirit who makes the Elect belong to him. By His Spirit's indwelling, Christ stakes His claim in the Elect as His possession, shares with them His righteousness which makes them pleasing to God, so that they who were bowed in the depths of sin can stand before Him. To the Old Testament lesson's promise of the Spirit to raise the dead, the epistle added the explanation of how God does this; then, through the Gospel, the Faithful showed the Elect a living picture of Christ's power to give life, proclaiming how He who raises from the spiritual death of sin, raises also from the physical death that is its terminal phase. Through the first reading the Faithful have portrayed for the Elect those spoken to and acted on by God who will know Him by His life-giving; in the psalm, the Faithful sang to them of waiting and dependence; and in the Gospel they have portrayed one who is raised by a God who weeps, who has His Spirit breathed into him and walks freely. Through these readings the Elect are told that God hears, that His Word has the power to bring life, that He seeks out the dead to raise them.

Taken together, the readings for the Third Scrutiny work to draw the Elect into the final time of purification remaining before their Baptism. In order for them to understand and be fully responsive to the grace that will be given to them there, the Elect must know both the depth of their own sinfulness and the immensity of God's mercy; thus, a major purpose of the scrutinies is to instruct the Elect gradually "about the mystery of sin, from which the whole world and every person longs to be delivered and thus saved from its present and future conse-

RCIA 143

quences." Through the readings of the scrutinies, the Elect are shown with increasing emphasis that whatever they are holding onto that is not God, but is more important to them than God, brings death, and so must be put to death. "From the first to the final scrutiny the Elect

RCIA 143

should progress in their perception of sin and their desire for salvation": the further the Elect go on their journey, the more the readings make them understand their need of Christ.

Thus, Psalm 130 is a realistic expression of the Elect's growing realization that they are dead in their sin, but that they may hope in the Word of Him who called forth Israel and Lazarus from their graves, and He will redeem them; it articulates well the prayer of those who, after many months of preparation, find themselves two weeks away from Baptism, and reminds the Elect that the precious gift of forgiveness, which they hear even the Faithful cry out for, is not to be taken for granted. And even as the readings of the Third Scrutiny bring into sharpest possible focus the Elect's need to turn from sin and surrender to God, they also emphasize the power God gives to enable that surrender, pointedly noting that the Spirit the Elect will receive at Baptism is the difference between death and life.

As the Elect move toward as complete a surrender of themselves to God as is possible for each of them at this point in their lives, the final obstacle hindering them from fully giving themselves may take many forms; perhaps the most difficult to overcome is a lack of trust occasioned by the Problem of Evil. Yet through the readings' insistent proclamation of God as One who brings life from death, good from evil, the Faithful can bear witness that even if the Elect's No to God is a refusal to trust they feel they must cling to in order to justify their pain, if they will bring the agonizing situation to Christ to resurrect in His time, in His way, He can raise them, too, from the mistrust that is killing them, cutting them off from the Love which is life.

True, to trust God, to love God, when God seems not to be God, is the ultimate death to self, but the Faithful make it clear that they have found that Christ gives them life not only in less serious difficulties, but even here in this ultimate death; they can testify that God will 1 Cor 10:13 not let the Elect be tried beyond their strength, but, with the trial, gives the means to endure it. And part of that means, the Faithful explain, comes through the Elect focussing their minds on what is true; they can look unremittingly at unjust suffering and eventually deny God, or they can turn their gaze to the God of infinite love and be empowered to give their lives to relieve suffering. If they are to learn the three-dimensional perception of faith, they must give their minds to thoughts of faith; to come to see as God sees, they must entertain the thoughts of those who see as God sees, which they find in His Word, and as they do this they will come to know the truth that can free them.

The Faithful know that to say Yes to God in the face of unjust evil, to say "I don't understand but I trust," is death—but they also know it is a Yes that has been said before, the Yes of the Cross, of One who was also abandoned, and entombed in death; His redemptive death and resurrection alone determine the meaning of things, for He alone is Life. To help the Elect discover this for themselves, the Faithful share with them instances they have known where people in the throes of unspeakable anguish at unjust evil that couldn't be healed by human means, have finally turned to the Redeeming Christ and found a reality of love they hadn't known existed, which makes all other loves seem flimsy, which brought fruit of life even from their pain. The question facing all those agonizing over the Problem of Evil is whether they will allow the deadly situation tormenting them, and themselves, dead in their separation from God because of it—to be Lazarus, to be raised, and to be "for the glory of God."

Even if many of the Elect have not yet personally wrestled with the Problem of Evil, the Faithful must not, in their preaching, avoid the Cross as part of the Christian life, for there is no resurrection without it, and it is not fair to leave converts unprepared; there are no guarantees that giving their lives to a God who is Love will keep them safe from all tragedy. Whether teaching on the Problem of Evil resonates in the Elect's experience today or not, at some point before Baptism the Faithful must plant it in their minds, so that it can come to them when they do need it, even if some of the meaning of their teaching may only become clear later as the Spirit reveals it; meanwhile, even if the Elect themselves are not struggling with senseless tragedy, the Faithful's teaching may help them comfort friends who do.

RCIA 141

[Progression of the three scrutinies]

The three scrutinies are intended to deepen the Elect's resolve "to carry out their decision to love God above all." Since this love is rooted in trust, the scrutinies have revealed to the Elect how their sin—the ways they say No to God—is ultimately refusal to trust, and the scrutiny readings summon the Elect to ever-deeper levels of trust: first, to trust God in the face of thirst, then to trust Him in the face of blindness, and finally to trust Him even in the face of death. The Elect are called to trust Christ as Living Water, and, when they cannot see how Christ is keeping His promise to be source of all they truly need, to learn to see differently and trust Christ as their perception in darkness; when, having learned to perceive through Christ's Light in ordinary frustrations, they are caught in a major agony where they cannot perceive how their experience is consistent with a loving God, they meet the ultimate test of trusting Christ as their perception. Here, they are called to be willing to trust Him to be their Life in death—to let go of all their defenses and idolatrous sources of worth, and die to all self-justification, trusting He will raise them, to say the ultimate Yes in the face of this annihilation; they are promised that at Baptism He will give them the Life that will enable them to overcome even this utter destruction. But the choice whether to trust is theirs; like the onlookers in today's Gospel, they can respond to Jesus' compassion by saying either, "See how He loves us" or, "If He loves us, why does He not show it the way we want Him to?"

RCIA 173

RCIA 152

If today's scrutiny has brought to light the ways the Elect need to trust God more deeply in the death of sin, or any kind of death, it has also revealed that they are willing to learn to trust, and so they are grateful when it is time for the community's intercession. "Elect of God, kneel down and pray." In the silence, the Faithful pray, as always, that the Elect will have a deeper understanding of their sin and a spirit of repentance, so they can enter into the true freedom of God's children; having learned that to the Yes of His love, there is no "Yes, but . . ."—

only Yes, or No—the Faithful pray that the Elect will allow that Yes continually to deepen in them. The Elect bring to God whatever expressions of their No may still keep them bound in death, and ask for Him to raise them: Lord, give us life, they pray.

RCIA 174

Rom 8:5

Then in the solemn intercessions, the Faithful petition their life-giving God for the specific graces they think will best prepare the Elect to be raised from death . . . May the Elect set their minds on the things of the Spirit, may they be attentive when the Spirit brings to mind the truth of the Word, so He can free them from the deadly tyranny of the flesh . . . May they continually remind themselves of the truths of why they trust and give thanks for the promise of salvation, so they can resist the snares of the Deceiver . . . May they have a horror of sin, so that they yearn to be raised . . . May the Elect, disintegrating in their No, be integrated by the life-giving Spirit of love . . . May they know Christ as Resurrection in whatever death they meet with, and be able to be comforted, to trust . . . As the Faithful pray, the Elect recall how Christ had promised to be their Living Water, had said He came to be their Light. "I will never fail you nor forsake you," He has said; hoping in His Word they continue to ask Him for life.

Deut 31:6,
Josh 1:5

RCIA 175

And now the Faithful, as so many times before, exercise the authority they have been given over anything that keeps the Elect bound up in their sin which is death. "Father of life. . ." The Elect think of how this Father sent His Son to snatch them from death's reign over them, how He wants to be glorified in raising them. "Free us," they pray, "from the Deceiver who ever prompts our race to speak the No to the Love-which-is-Life, which keeps us wasting in sin's death; then let us bear witness, even as your Faithful, to how you raised us from our death of No." "Lord Jesus . . ." "Your Word pulled Lazarus from the tomb, to show you turn evil to glory, death to abundance of life. Come to us enshrouded in our No and help us trust your Word; then in the waters let your Spirit fill us with your life, so we can know in our flesh the glory of the Resurrection." "For you are Lord, forever and ever." "Yes, we will trust you to be our very life." "Amen." And as they lie sealed in the cave of their deadly sin, hoping in His Word, they feel its resonance in the dark air around them. "The hour is coming, and soon is here, when the dead will hear the voice of the Son of God, and those who hear will live; for it is not by measure that I give my Spirit."

John 5:25;
3:34

"Thy Strong
Word," M.
Franzmann

So now the Elect must keep on waiting, with more longing than watchmen for daybreak, for that strong Word that will cleave the darkness of their No and brand them with the life-giving Spirit of Christ's Yes, that will raise them from their graves of sin and bring them home into the land of God's People, the Church. In this time of promises and warnings the Elect have been promised that by the love of the Father,

Christ will give them a resurrection from sin that is the pledge of resurrection from sin's consequence, death; they have been warned that sharing in Christ's resurrection does not eliminate from their lives the deadly evils their No brought into the world, but redeems them. "Dear Elect, go in peace. May the Lord remain with you always."

RCIA 176

"Amen"; the rite is over, but the waiting still goes on. They came dead in sin's exile from the kingdom of love which is their true home; they leave hoping in a life-giving Word of promise still ringing in their ears: "Did I not tell you that if you believed, you would see the glory of God?"

John 11:40

VII. The Presentation of the Lord's Prayer

"Thus, with the catechumenal formation of the elect completed, the Church lovingly entrusts to them the Creed and the Lord's Prayer, the ancient texts that have always been regarded as expressing the heart of the Church's faith and prayer. These texts are presented in order to enlighten the elect. . . . The Lord's Prayer fills them with a deeper realization of the new spirit of adoption by which they will call God their Father, especially in the midst of the eucharistic assembly" (no. 147).

RCIA	*Lectionary*
nos. 21, 138–139, 147–149, 178–184	Hos 11:1b, 3-4, 8c-9
	Ps 103:1-2, 8, 10, 11-12, 13, 18
	(or Ps 23:1-3a, 3b-4, 5, 6; see Scrutiny II)
	Rom 8:14-17, 26-27
	(or Gal 4:4-7)
	Matt 6:9-13

Note: In the epistle St. Paul tells Christians that God has made them *huioi* (sons) of God by giving them a spirit of *huiothesia* (being put in the place of a son, as in adoption). In Paul's time, daughters did not enjoy the same status as sons, so when he speaks of all who are led by the Spirit (men *and* women) as sons of God, he is affirming that men and women are of equal worth with each other in their relationship with God. As he explains in Gal 3:26-28: "In Christ Jesus you are all sons of God through faith. For as many of you as were baptized in Christ have put on Christ. There is neither Jew nor Greek, there is neither slave nor free, there is neither male nor female; for you are all one in Christ Jesus."

In the commentary I have spoken of the baptized as God's "children" or "heirs" wherever possible. However, since "children" can connote immaturity, and the meaning of heirs is limited to "those who get something," in some cases I have continued to speak of Baptism as making Christians sons of God. Following Paul's word-use also makes it clear that the "spirit of sonship" Christians receive at Baptism is in fact the Spirit of *the* Son, Jesus Christ. When Christians receive the Holy Spirit at Baptism, they are united to Christ by receiving His own Spirit; thus identified with Christ, they share in His sonship in a way that transcends gender.

And so they have continued to wait, learning to allow their trust to deepen that God will be true to His Word, and rescue them from any death that hinders them from entering into the Life He would give them, the only life that matters. It is good that the Elect have this time before their Baptism to learn to wait for God's Word, for afterwards there will be other times, lasting longer than this, when they will have

Rom 8:25

to wait for Him, to hope for what they do not see and so wait for it with patience. Then they will remember how this waiting before Baptism taught them trust, and they will be able to wait in hope again,

Rom 5:5

and once more find their hope is not disappointed.

The Elect have seen how becoming ever more aware of their need of God has forced them to trust Him more, and how that trust has made them more open to Him, more vulnerable to Him than they have ever been before. Whatever Word the Faithful deliver to them today through this final rite, it will touch them at the heart of who they are as they come before God. Their waiting has carved out a deep silence in them,

1 Sam 3:10

in just the right shape to receive whatever Word will be spoken. "Speak, Lord," they pray in their hearts; "speak, Lord, your servant is listening."

> Thus says the LORD:
> When Israel was a child, I loved him,
>   and out of Egypt I called my son.
> Yet it was I who taught Ephraim to walk;
>   I took them up in my arms;
>   but they did not know that I healed them.
> I led them with cords of compassion,
>   with the bands of love,
> and I became to them as one
>   who eases the yoke on their jaws,
>   and I bent down to them and fed them.
> My heart recoils within me,
>   my compassion grows warm and tender.
> I will not execute my fierce anger,
>   I will not again destroy Ephraim;
> for I am God and not man,
>   the Holy One in your midst,

Hos 11:1b,
3-4, 8c-9

> and I will not come to destroy.

After all that emphasis on death to self in the final scrutiny, as the Elect opened their hearts to receive God's Word through the first reading, they had been expecting a dramatic symphony of demands for self-immolation to come rushing into their silence, overwhelming it. But instead there is simply a single pure voice, ringing clear and true: God singing of how He has loved His People whom He called even as a child, and how this love reveals who He is. From the beginning He has cared for them: holding out His arms and encouraging them to come to Him in their first tottering steps, embracing them and carrying them when the way was too hard for them to walk, healing them when they were too young to comprehend how He was preserving them. He raised them, formed them as a People by the way of love, stooped down from His omnipotence to feed them. And when His People grew to be rebellious, He did not annihilate them with the force of His just anger; because of who He is—His holiness—He will never destroy them.

The Elect think back to the very first rite of their catechumenate, when they heard of God's call to Abram, and reflect on all they have learned since of how God has called a People to belong to Him. They see how the Faithful surrounding them this day are, like Israel, those adopted by God, who have come to know Him as Hosea has described Him, and in whose midst He dwells as Holy One; and they, too—the Elect—are called out of Egypt to join this People on whom God bestows filial adoption. What a mystery, they think: here, so close to the destination of their pilgrimage, the All-Powerful One they sought so long shows Himself to them simply as Father; the final Word He gives them as journeybread is that He has always loved them, been with them, cared for them, leading them every step as they sought after Him, even though they didn't know it or appreciate it. Today He simply reaffirms to the Elect that He has called them from bondage to sonship, emphasizing what He has told them all along of how tenderly He would take care of them, of the warmth of His compassion. Like Israel long ago and the Faithful today, the Elect may well deserve to be destroyed by His wrath for the willful rebellion of their sin that has become so painfully clear to them during this Lenten time of purification, they realize—but He turns from His anger and accepts them as His own child. There is no word for it but mystery; and the opposite extremes between which the Elect have learned to chart their journey are not difficult to find: unredeemed humanity, with its penchant for angry destruction, and the God who is Holy, who makes a compassionate commitment not to destroy. "I will not execute my fierce anger, I will not again destroy Ephraim; for I am God and not man, the Holy One in your midst, and I will not come to destroy."

The Elect want to give voice to their gratitude for this Word God has spoken, and to be able to keep it alive in their minds during the final days before their Baptism; as always, the Faithful have anticipated their need.

Ps 103:13   ℟ As a father is kind to his children,
so kind is the Lord to those who fear him.

Bless the Lord, O my soul;
    and all that is within me bless his holy name!
Bless the Lord, O my soul,
    and forget not all his benefits.

The Lord is merciful and gracious,
    slow to anger and abounding in steadfast love.
He does not deal with us according to our sins,
    nor requite us according to our iniquities.

For as the heavens are high above the earth,
    so great is his steadfast love toward those who fear him;
as far as the east is from the west,
    so far does he remove our transgressions from us.

As a father pities his children,
    so the Lord pities those who fear him,
Those who keep his covenant
    and remember to do his commandments.

Ps 103:1-2,
8, 10, 11-12,
13, 18

The language of worship, since it is the language of love, is a language of repetition, and in the psalm the Faithful invite the Elect to listen once more to truths they have heard from the beginning, and affirm their desire to be penetrated by the reality of these truths. This

Ps 103:19

God whose throne is in the heavens, whose kingdom rules over all, approaches His People as Father, enveloping them in a steadfast love that extends as far as the distance between the heavens and earth; He whose name—the deepest reality of who He is—is so holy it is to be blessed unceasingly with every part of their being, reaches out to draw His People to Him in mercy and grace. And the Faithful they will soon

Ps 103:20-21

join, the Elect see, are those who with the mighty angels bless this God. They have learned that to grow in their love of God, and their knowledge of His love, they must call to mind His kindnesses to them and thank Him for them; they remember every one of His gifts to them, and recall each by name to stir up their love. He has not punished them as their sins deserved, but simply taken their sins away. As they have sought to fear Him, to be Faithful to His covenant and commandments, He has looked on them with the heartfelt compassion of a father for his children.

And this God is promising the Elect to be as kind to them, too, as a Father to His children. Even as they come before Him this day, aware as never before of the depth and seriousness of their sin, He promises to respond with overflowing mercy, to remove their sins as far as east

Ps 34:11

from west. As in the first psalm they sang as catechumens, so many months ago, the Faithful had urged the Elect to come and learn the fear of the Lord, so now in the psalm of this final rite, the Faithful again exhort the Elect to fear Him, to honor Him, and they remind them of how to behave as a child of God: to praise Him and bless His holy name; the Faithful invite the Elect, whose adoption as God's children will so soon be complete, to join them in continually proclaiming His benefits to them, how He is slow to anger and abounds in faithful love. As the Elect hear themselves encouraged to renew their decision to live in covenant with God and obey Him, they hear also the contrasts between west, and east; sin and iniquity, and the Lord's mercy and gracious love. "As a father is kind to his children, so kind is the Lord to those who fear him."

Clearly, think the Elect, through His Word proclaimed to them today, God is seeking to deepen their understanding of how He would be to them as Father. But so far they have heard mostly about the Father's part of this relationship; what is it like to be the child of such a Father?

> All who are led by the Spirit of God are sons of God. For you did not receive the spirit of slavery to fall back into fear, but you have received the spirit of sonship. When we cry, "Abba! Father!" it is the Spirit himself bearing witness with our spirit that we are children of God, and if children, then heirs, heirs of God and fellow heirs with Christ, provided we suffer with him in order that we may also be glorified with him.
>
> Likewise the Spirit helps us in our weakness; for we do not know how to pray as we ought, but the Spirit himself intercedes for us with sighs too deep for words. And he who searches the hearts of men knows what is the mind of the Spirit, because the Spirit intercedes for the saints according to the will of God.

Rom 8:14-17, 26-27

At the final scrutiny last Sunday, the Faithful invited the Elect to hear with them Paul's explanation of how the Spirit God promised to give them at Baptism would work in them to change their self-seeking behavior; now they show the Elect how Paul goes on to explain that the Spirit is able to transform their behavior because His indwelling effects the ever-deeper transformation of their very identity. For this Spirit God will give them, which will change the way they conduct their lives, does not simply issue commands, coercing them to scramble to obey like slaves, whose every thought and deed is motivated by fear. No, the Faithful have discovered, God does not bring about their obedience to His love by filling them with a spirit of compulsion, but rather with a spirit of adoption, inspiring their thinking and actions with the awareness of their identity as His children, and the loving desire to obey. After their Easter Baptism, the world may recognize as fact that the Elect have been baptized because they possess a paper document, imprinted with a notary's seal; but the Elect themselves will know because they will experience the Spirit's seal on their hearts, making them children of God, which He bears witness to each time they turn to God as Father. And since they *are* His children, God gives them a claim to all His riches, even as He shared them with His Son who is first-born of the many brethren. To receive their inheritance the Elect must simply live out their identity as His children, and willingly bear whatever suffering this obedience brings them, as Christ has already done, so that God can reveal the shining of Christ's faithfulness in them.

This Spirit of adoption the Elect will receive does not simply label them as sons, the Faithful insist, but actually effects in them all the aspects of childrens' relationship with their Father. For the Faithful have learned that of themselves they do not know how children of such a Father speak to Him. They know they must ask Him for all that His love wants to give them, but it is so glorious there are no words for it in their language; and they do not know what earthly circumstances would help bring it about, so they don't even know what ordinary things to pray for. But the Faithful have found the Spirit helping them in their weakness, praying within them, asking God for whatever is truly good for them, in a prayer that is richer than words could express; even if the Faithful don't comprehend this prayer, they know their Father does, for it is His Spirit He breathed into them who prays, asking of God what God so desires to give.

As the Faithful present Paul's teaching that when at Baptism the Elect are adopted as sons, they will be given God's Spirit that makes them sons, they know the Elect have heard these concepts before. Somehow the Faithful must make it clear that this spirit of sonship the Elect will receive is not a matter of words—a matter of calling themselves sons, pretending to be sons, although nothing in them has changed. No, when they are reborn in Baptism, the Elect will experience a new identity coming to life in them, the true identity they began to journey toward in the first rite of the catechumenate; they will discover that whatever unique gifts have been given them, their fundamental identity is as children of God.

Gal 4:5

Perhaps they had been struggling with the fear that their Yes to God at Baptism would destroy them, so that they were no longer themselves; they will find that this is true in the sense that the bondage to self-obsession which characterized the personalities that they had called "themselves" *is* destroyed, and replaced with the freedom of the Spirit of Christ, the Spirit of the Son of the heavenly Father. Then they will understand that, faithful to His promise, God will not come to destroy the true selves they were created to be, but only the sin that has disfigured His image in them. And when God has washed off the rebellion that mars them, with His Spirit He will emblazon in them the icon, the royal image of His Son, luminous with the vivid hues of filial faithfulness and love.

As the Faithful seek to convey Paul's word to the Elect in a way that makes it come alive for them, the Elect perceive that the Faithful are speaking of what they know. They *are* led by the Spirit they speak of, and so they are sons of God, animated by the spirit of sonship, true heirs with Christ; they are those helped by the Spirit in their weakness, those for whom He intercedes, saints—holy ones—made holy by this Holy Spirit. And all that the Faithful have described will soon be bestowed on the Elect. If they are willing to be so united to Christ that they share with Him the suffering that faithfulness to the Father costs, they too will be heirs of God and share in His glory; they too will be led by the Spirit, counted among the saints. As they continue the journey toward their adoption the Elect see, as always, that their way lies between pairs of opposites: a spirit of slavery, characterized by fear, and the spirit of sonship which trustfully knows God as "Abba"; suffering with Christ, and being glorified with Him. "And He who searches the hearts of men knows what is the mind of the Spirit, because the Spirit intercedes for the saints according to the will of God."

So close to the end of their journey, the Elect are no longer demanding answers to specific questions. "Come, Holy Spirit, help us; give us whatever we need to approach God as our Father and to live as His faithful children."

RCIA 180   "Let those who are to receive the Lord's Prayer now come forward."

Rom 8:15   ℣ You have received the Spirit which makes us God's children,
                   and in that Spirit we call God our Father.

Jesus was praying in a certain place, and when he ceased, one of his disciples said to him, "Lord, teach us to pray, as John taught his disciples." And he said to them, "When you pray, say:
     Our Father who art in heaven,
     Hallowed be thy name.
     Thy kingdom come,
     Thy will be done,
          On earth as it is in heaven.
     Give us this day our daily bread;
     And forgive us our trespasses,
          As we forgive those who trespass against us;

Luke 11:1-2a   And lead us not into temptation,
Matt 6:9b-13   But deliver us from evil."

They should be used to it by now—the deacon turns the page and there is Jesus. The Elect had known, of course, that at today's rite the

Lord's Prayer would be presented to them, but it had not occurred to them that this would happen during the Gospel; they had assumed it would be like when they received the Creed: after the readings the Faithful would present it on behalf of the entire Church by reciting it to them. But instead Christ Himself gives it to them through the Gospel; in this final Gospel before the Rites of Preparation, this prayer is the Spirit's answer to the Elect's petition for whatever they most need to know.

Why? As the Elect ponder this simple prayer seeking to understand why it is so important, they begin to see that if they contemplated it for the rest of their lives, if they were as holy as the holiest saints, they could still never fathom the fullness of its meaning, for each petition embodies a truth of infinite depth. So far today the Faithful have spoken to them of how God is their Father who gives them His Spirit to make them His children. Now the Elect reflect that this Spirit of sonship is the Spirit of Jesus, the Only-Begotten Son, who thus shares with these created sons His relationship with His Father. And in this Gospel the true Son is teaching them, the adopted ones, how children of the Father pray to Him, how they relate to Him as Father, what they say to Him with their lives. He shows them that the heart of the relationship of a loving son to his Father, is to want what the Father most wants, to desire it more than anything, and to live this desire in all their actions and their words. As He offers them this prayer, the Elect seek to pray each petition with Him, as He has given them to understand it so far.

". . . Hallowed be thy name. . ." May You who are Love, be loved and praised. May You be glorified in Your children's becoming resplendent with Your love as You created us to be; may You be glorified in our allowing Your love to blaze through us, drawing all the world into the fire of Your compassion. . . .

"Thy kingdom come, Thy will be done, On earth as it is in heaven. . ." (What does it mean to pray for the coming of the kingdom of One whose kingdom "rules over all"? the Elect once wondered . . .) May Your reign be firmly established in us, may we abdicate as pretenders to Your throne, and be ruled by Your grace . . . May Your reign be established, Your will be fulfilled over all realms on earth, throughout all creation—crushing hatred and war, smashing oppression and lies . . . (The Elect reflect that to pray this prayer sincerely and with fervor is a more subversive act than any demonstration of social protest one could engage in . . .)

"Give us this day our daily bread . . ." So often we have complained we don't have more than we do, but now we see everything we have and use each day, *everything* we need to sustain our lives in any way, comes from You; we must ask You for it in expression of

Ps 103:19

our utter dependence. And even more than the bread of our mundane needs, we depend on You to provide us with the bread that feeds our spirit, in Your Word and at Your table . . . Lord, give us all that we need this day to live out our love for You. . .

"And forgive us our trespasses, as we forgive those who trespass against us . . ." How strongly the Faithful have emphasized the importance of forgiveness—ever pointing out to the Elect, from the very beginning of their catechumenate, that they are asking God to forgive the incalculable debt they owe Him, according as they have forgiven the wrongs committed against them! It was one thing when they were simply learning to swallow their pride, when the one who sinned against them acknowledged the wrong, was sincerely sorry, and asked forgiveness. It was another, when the Faithful had insisted the Elect must forgive even when the person involved refused to admit their wrong; yet, even here, the Elect had come to see that if they nurtured a self-righteous desire to get even, they were no better than those who wronged them, and they learned to forgive here, too.

But then, what about those times when serious harm is caused to them by one who won't acknowledge it and doesn't care, when the Elect's lack of forgiveness manifests itself not in arrogant anger but in an inability to let go of the hurt, allowing it to ferment very slowly into resentment and bitterness? How is it humanly possible to "let go of" serious wrongs? And how can a God who claims to love the Elect expect them to ask that He forgive them, as they have already forgiven those who brought such crippling pain into their lives and are unrepentant?

Patiently, the Faithful have explained (as it had to be patiently explained to them) that God tells His People to pray in this way not to punish them for their lack of forgiveness, adding to the pain of the wrong they already suffer the pain of God's refusing to forgive *them*. No, the loving Father tells His children to let go of others' sin, stop clutching it to themselves, toying with it in their minds, because He knows sin is more dangerous than radioactive waste; He wants His children to stop holding onto others' sin against them and give it to Him because He is the only one who can properly dispose of it. Their self-justification in clinging to how others have wronged them will not restore the balance of justice in the universe: only Christ on the Cross can do that; they may as well try to clean up radioactive waste with their bare hands. It is not for humankind to try to do what only God can do: deal with the horror of sin; children of the Father must accept the fact that others' sin is too dangerous for them to play with, and surrender it to Him to be nailed to the Cross and destroyed. God's forgiveness of the Elect depends on their forgiveness of others, because if their hands are fully occupied with justifying themselves by holding onto others' sin, their hands will not be free for Him to grasp them and pull them up into the embrace of His forgiving love, which alone justifies their worth.

And when Jesus tells them to ask for forgiveness as they have already forgiven, He is not demanding the impossible. True, sometimes a wrong is so serious, that it feels like "letting go" of it is denying how serious it is or the harm it caused, and that the agony of this denial will destroy them. But even here the Faithful have found that if they bring the wrong to Christ who lives in them by His Spirit, He will forgive it in them, and bring them through the "death" of this forgiveness to a purer life of love. ". . . Father, forgive us and help us forgive," pray the Elect.

"And lead us not into temptation, but deliver us from evil. . ." "When we come up against things that challenge our faith, our love, free us from our fascination with the Deceiver's suggestions of how to respond to these things that try us. Give us your strength so the temptations we encounter will be as tests we passed, not seductions we entered into. Give us your grace," they pray.

When the Elect had heard that the purpose of this final rite before their Baptism was to present them with the Lord's Prayer, they had felt it was anticlimactic: they learned this prayer by heart a long time ago, they had been praying it for months, it's even part of the Rosary— why had the Faithful waited so long to formally present it to them? they had wondered. But as they have stood listening to Christ teach this prayer to them, they have found themselves more aware of how its power is not as properly recited formula, but as articulation of the life of a faithful son. It is therefore the prayer par excellence of the Church, which she prays unfailingly when she comes into the presence of the One who has called her together, when she stands before Him in her most solemn act of prayer and thanksgiving. And it is a prayer of the Church as community; by praying *"Our* Father" the Faithful give expression to the fact that they always pray as part of the whole Church God has redeemed.

As those who are not yet of the Faithful, the Elect may never have been present when the Church prayed this prayer. They reflect that perhaps the Creed, though it seems more difficult, was presented to them first because, more doctrinal, it helps unite them to the Church as People; the Lord's Prayer, more personal, welcomes them into the Church as family. The Creed the Elect will "give back" by professing it *for* the Faithful on the morning of Holy Saturday; but they will not "give back" the Lord's Prayer until they have received the Spirit of adoption in Baptism, enabling them truly to address God as Father as full members of His Church, and so pray *"Our* Father" *with* the Faithful immediately before their first Communion with the Church at the Easter Vigil. It is fitting, then, that the Faithful have waited until now solemnly to present to the Elect the more familiar language used by those adopted as God's children when they come before Him as family.

In this Gospel, then, Jesus is instructing the Elect that they must learn to pray as *He* teaches them—a prayer that is prayed with their lives as well as their words, and that is prayed in union with the community of disciples He calls—and He is entrusting to them the prayer He gives to His disciples. The Faithful are this community who ever pray this prayer He taught them, God's children who know they depend on Him for sustenance, forgiveness, guidance, and protection, who day by day seek His kingdom. "Give us this day our daily bread; and forgive us our trespasses as we forgive those who trespass against us; and lead us not into temptation, but deliver us from evil."

[Relationship of readings to each other]
In the silence as the assembly absorbs God's Word to them through the readings and the homily, the Elect consider what the Faithful have proclaimed to them. Through the reading from Hosea the Faithful had confessed that even they had not always heeded God, but that He had taught them, and revealed Himself to them as a People, as Father. Having invited the Elect through this reading to join them in identifying with the wayward child Israel, on whom the Lord had not executed His anger as he deserved, the Faithful then led them in the psalm in a fitting prayer for that child, describing the many dimensions of God's paternal care; the Faithful know that the Elect need to learn to speak *of* how God is like a Father (as in the psalm) before they will be able to speak *to* Him as Father (as in the Gospel). Then, after the epistle told the Elect *that* God's Spirit He will give them will make them sons of God, the Gospel showed them *how:* what it is that the Spirit prays in them which they must allow to be incarnated in their daily lives. Having instructed the Elect in the psalm to "bless His holy name," in the Gospel the Faithful give them a prayer in which they do, the perfect prayer of "those who fear Him." The Gospel of the Lord's Prayer is thus the icon of the relationship with God described by the preceding readings—the prayer of a beloved heir who expects mercy.

[Relationship of rite and faith-experience]
Through the readings, the Faithful provide the Elect with what they need for the last stage of their journey. The Faithful know that to prepare for Baptism it is necessary to have not only a deep awareness of sin, which is evoked by the scrutinies, but also to recall God's goodness and forgiving nature; two of today's readings speak of God not dealing with His People as they deserve, and the Lord's Prayer provides the Elect with the opportunity to express their trust in His forgiveness. The Rite of the Presentation of the Lord's Prayer is intended

RCIA 147

to enlighten the Elect "with a deeper realization of the spirit of adoption by which they will call God their Father"; all of its readings speak of the Elect's adoption as sons of a loving Father: who teaches His children to walk, who makes them His heirs and gives them His Spirit as a pledge, and who forgives their sins. The Elect will be able to keep pondering the message of these readings in the days to come as they sing to themselves the psalm refrain, which is almost a summary of the readings.

Since the Elect can only learn to address God as Father from those who already do, as the Presentation of the Profession of Faith gave ritual enactment to the role of the Faithful in teaching the Elect the doctrinal truths of the Church, so the Presentation of the Lord's Prayer enacts their role in teaching the Elect to pray (which they fulfill by bringing them to Christ who alone can teach them). The Faithful not only

RCIA 147

offer them the actual words that are the heart of the prayer of the Church but also promise the Spirit who will give those words a living meaning, and who, when they need it, will pray in them a prayer too deep for words; the Spirit of sonship is also the Spirit of perfect worship.

The closer the Elect have come to Baptism, the more the Faithful have told them about this Spirit they will receive there. From the men-

Rom 5:5

tion in the First Scrutiny of the Spirit pouring God's love into their hearts, the Faithful have gone on to explain how the Spirit can change the way the Elect perceive things, and actually transform their behavior, leading them in a way of life that is radically different, because it is Christ-like. In today's rite, the Faithful's increasing openness concerning this Spirit reaches a climax: those who *are* led by the Spirit are actually sons of God. The Faithful know how crucial it is that the Elect be informed of all that God longs to do for them through the Spirit, for only to the extent they know such gifts are possible and confidently expect them, will they be able to receive them. The "delay" of the Elect's "giving back" the Lord's Prayer until the Eucharist *after* their Baptism is not an over-literalistic formality; it is the expression of the profound theological truth of how the Church is constituted and enabled to call on God as Father by the Spirit, and a pastoral insistence that the Elect's reception of the Spirit in the font is not a technical term for an intellectual theory, but something that actually happens. "From antiquity the Lord's Prayer has been the prayer proper to those who in Baptism have received the spirit of adoption. When the Elect have been baptized and take part in their first celebration of the Eucharist, they will join the

RCIA 149

rest of the Faithful in saying the Lord's Prayer."

Perhaps it gave the Elect pause, as they realized that they would not be able to pray the Lord's Prayer (which they may be used to "rattling off") formally, liturgically, until they are adopted, with the rest of God's adopted children. Now they reflect that it is the Spirit bearing witness that they are God's children who is the source of the family resemblance in all the Faithful, as He forms each of them through this prayer in the image of the faithful Son; and, as the Spirit brings out in each one the image of Christ, He forms them all as Body of Christ, chosen to bear the likeness of the Son, lovingly calling on God as Father.

Rom 8:29

RCIA 182

"Let us pray for these Elect. . ."

The Faithful pray the Elect will have the grace they need in the days of waiting left, to leave behind slavery and fear and prepare for the Spirit of sons: the Spirit of power and love and self-control, who gives the ability to be Faithful. As they listen, the Elect remember how, when they arrived today, all they could think of was death and destruction. But His name is not Destroyer—He only destroys to make new: the One they will say Yes to is Father.

2 Tim 1:7

". . . Give them new birth in your living waters, so that they may be numbered among your adopted children. We ask this through Christ our Lord. Amen."

RCIA 183

"Dear Elect, go in peace, and may the Lord remain with you always."

"Amen," and, with new confidence, they go. They came this day fearing to cast themselves into a pit of self-annihilation; they leave knowing they will hurl themselves into their Father's arms.

Summary: The Rites of the Scrutinies and Presentations

RCIA 139

The Rite of Election introduced the newly Elect into the time of purification and enlightenment, "a period of more intense spiritual preparation" before their Baptism, which normally takes place during Lent. Since Lent is the season when the Church prepares for its solemn celebration of the Paschal Mystery, which is the heart of its life, it is a season of conversion, both for those who will be plunged into the mystery of Christ's saving death and resurrection at Baptism and for the Faithful, who seek to allow that mystery to permeate their lives more completely; the many descriptions of the life of the baptized in the liturgy during Lent provide the Faithful with reminders of the splendor of their calling in light of which they can examine their lives, and, simultaneously, deepen the Elect's understanding of the life for which they are preparing.

RCIA 138

The conversion the Elect must experience during this time is a *metanoia*—a changing of their minds—which is not a matter of learning new doctrines (doctrinal formation must be completed before they can be admitted to the Elect), but of allowing their minds to be more deeply penetrated and formed by the truths of Christian revelation. The Elect must seriously consider to what extent the death and resurrection of Christ they will be united to at Easter is actually the central determining reality of their lives; to what extent, for example, does it inform their behavior in relationship to the three aspects of life which may be seen as symbolized in the Gospel at the Rite of Election: material possessions, human relationships, and power? To what extent do the truths revealed in Scripture inform their thoughts—how do they use their minds all day? The Elect, though not crippled by serious sin, seek a deeper conversion by searching for ways that their thinking and behavior is not shaped by the Gospel, praying for the grace to change, and changing. Yet while the Faithful encourage this growth in self-knowledge, they ensure that it is aimed not at the dead-end of introspection, but at contemplation of the Paschal Mystery and its consequences; the purpose of this time of examination of conscience and penance is "to enlighten the minds and hearts of the Elect with a deeper knowledge of Christ the Savior."

RCIA 142

RCIA 139

RCIA 139

The central locus of the Elect's conversion during this time of purification and enlightenment is the liturgical assembly, primarily the rites of the scrutinies and presentations. The scrutinies are celebrated at the Eucharists of the third, fourth, and fifth Sundays of Lent, with the proper readings for Year A; they comprise these readings, solemn intercessions by the Faithful with laying on of hands by godparents, exorcism, and formal dismissal of the Elect before the Prayer of the

Faithful. During the scrutinies the Elect come into the presence of the Word proclaimed to discover what is revealed, in light of that Word, concerning what aspects of their lives need repentance and healing, and what aspects should be encouraged and strengthened; as the Spirit works through the proclamation of the Word, and through the community's prayer and exorcism, to evoke conviction of sin and repentance, the Elect are freed from the hold sin and Satan have on them, find new strength in Christ against temptation, and deepen their decision to love

RCIA 141   God over all.

Since it is not possible for people to perceive everything they need to repent of all at once, and since some ways that conversion is necessary cannot be understood until others are dealt with (and if they were even perceived at the beginning, the Elect might be scared away from entering into the conversion process!), there is a gradual progression in the call to repentance from the First to the Third Scrutiny. Through the scrutinies the Elect are confronted in increasingly stronger doses

RCIA 143   both with the seriousness of human sin and need for salvation, and with the fact that there is a Savior. The scrutinies are intended to evoke in the Elect an increasingly deeper recognition of how they resist God's saving love, and a correspondingly deeper experience of the power of the Cross to transform them; the more thoroughly the Elect perceive their need for redemption and desire and pray for it, the more thoroughly, by grace, can they change.

As the Rite of Election, regardless of which set of readings is used, must strongly present the Gospel of salvation in Christ, so each scrutiny must deepen the Elect's knowledge of that Gospel; if the Rite of Election shows them what they are saved *from* (sin, death, and Satan), the scrutinies show them what they are saved *for* (union with Christ who is Living Water, Light, and Life). Whatever the Elect may have thought their problem was (if they thought they had one) when they began to investigate Christianity, it must now be made unmistakably clear that the *real* problem is sin; if they had once thought that the good news was that if they went through the motions of Church membership God would give them everything they wanted, now they know that it is that they can live a different way, freed from sin's tyranny. The scrutinies convince the Elect that they *need* a Savior much more than they had thought, and that Christ *is* a Savior much more than they had thought; the more deeply they desire Christ as Redeemer, the more deeply they can receive Him as Redeemer. Thus the scrutinies, through their Scripture readings, preaching, prayer, and exorcism, function sacramentally: both expressing the Elect's need for purification and enlightenment, and working to effect it through the power of the proclamation of Christ as Living Water, Light, and Life.

There are many ways the proper readings of the scrutinies may be treated in preaching in order to "instruct the Elect gradually about the mystery of sin." The first reading of the First Scrutiny suggests that one way the Elect can examine their lives to discover "what is weak, defective, or sinful" is by considering to what extent they actually trust God. While the converts' catechumenate began with the reading of Abram setting out in trust on a journey to a place unknown, their time of purification and enlightenment as Elect catechumens begins with the children of Israel complaining and doubting God's care for them on *their* journey. As children learn to walk by falling as well as by keeping their balance, so the Elect can learn through their occasional missteps how to walk in faith, and depending too much on their spontaneous feelings about things rather than trusting God, is a common source of stumbling. It is thus appropriate that the Elect's forty days (not years) of wilderness training begin with scrutiny of their trust in God's providence. Further, as the Elect learn to rely on God to provide for them, and to live in thankfulness for all He gives, they can also consider how He calls them to use it; those who have come to know Christ as Living Water are those who willingly share with those in need, not simply of their excess, but of their substance as well.

RCIA 141

It is possible, then, to understand the First Scrutiny as reminding the Elect that the divine compassion is poured into the world as Living Water, and that as this water flows through them, they are to respond in a life that is an incarnate thank-you, and as generous stewards of whatever resources are given them. When the Elect first realize that this is in fact what life is about, that all they must do is let go and say Yes to such mercy, it seems to solve everything, but inevitably they will run up against problems. In the Rite of Election they were warned that they still entertained the delusion that they were the center of the universe; the readings of the Second Scrutiny can be seen as inviting them to consider how deeply this delusion affects their perception.

At the very first rite of the catechumenate, when the converts' senses were signed with the Cross, they were invited to learn a new way of seeing, but the further they go on their journey, the more they will realize how their whole manner of perceiving needs to change. As they begin to be enlightened by faith, and to experience "a progressive change in outlook," the converts do leave behind the manifest "works of darkness," but in order to continue "walking in the light" they must go further, and learn to see with Christ's eyes, to see by Christ as Light. They must be willing to let go of their instantaneous evaluation of things, their "right" to sit as judge of people and situations. Further, there will be times when what they see apparently contradicts what they believe. Here they must be able to realize that human natural perception can be so distorted and false as to be blindness, and that people encourage

RCIA 75.2

this blindness in each other; they must know that they are blind, must want to see as God sees, and turn to Christ for light, knowing that He will give it.

Even now the Elect must learn that those who truly see are those who do not seek to impose their own view of reality even on God, but those who, in trust, perceive everything through God's love for them and others. For the Elect to have "their spirit filled with Christ the Redeemer, who is . . . the light of the world" is for them to know that by Christ the Light in them, they will be able to see the Father as Christ does; to pray as those who see, is to trust.

RCIA 143

Thus, the readings of the First Scrutiny can be presented so as to enable the Elect to come to a deeper dependence on God's providence and a resolution to "give thanks in all circumstances," and those of the Second can be presented to confront them with the serious need for healing in their perception. But the contrast between opposite pairs of images that characterizes the scrutinies is drawn in ever-sharper terms: dryness and water, darkness and light, death and life; the proper readings of the Third Scrutiny proclaim unflinchingly that sin is death, physical and spiritual. If, after the first two scrutinies, the Elect are willing, by grace, to accept God as source and as perception, in what way might they still be separated from God by sin which is serious enough to be imaged by death?

1 Thess 5:18

There are many ways to present the readings of the Third Scrutiny to convince that sin is death and Christ is life. Since at the heart of human sin is the desire to be God—to determine what happens and what it means—any conscious rebellion can be deadly. However, the point at which this rebellion often makes its last stand, even in people who are quite dedicated to God in most areas of their lives, is in unwillingness to trust when confronted by unjust suffering; the Problem of Evil is the ultimate reminder that one is not God, that God is God, can allow what He wants and say what it means, and is who He says He is even when everything contradicts that. The temptation here even for exemplary believers, is to feel that God, by not rectifying whatever is causing their pain, is denying their worth, and that they must hold fast their anger and bitterness to be able to believe they are worth anything at all; yet this very refusal to trust separates them from God, who alone can bring them healing. To say Yes to God completely, as all Christians hope to do, is to say that the love of God poured out in Christ is enough; it is only in wrestling with the Problem of Evil that some faithful Christians—if they are honest—may discover it is not enough. Then they must ask God to change their hearts so that God's love is enough for them; they must enter into the mystery that God's love and God's will are the same, and must accept Christ in His death and resurrection as the source of meaning through which all things are understood, rather than their unredeemed nature. The Problem of Evil is real and should not be denied, but Christ can raise believers even from its deadly grip of refusal to trust. One way that the readings of the Third Scrutiny can be presented, then, is to encourage the Elect to die the death of wanting to be God, and thus to desire to seek and be formed by God's understanding of things, not their own determinations.

RCIA 143 In instructing the Elect "gradually about the mystery of sin," the three scrutiny Gospels manifest a progressive bluntness about the Elect's condition: first, they are told they are thirsty, then, that they are blind, then, that they are dead and there is a good chance that they stink; in order to come to life they must first know how dead they are. The sequence of these stories also evidences an increasing frankness about the cost of responding to Jesus' Word: the Samaritan Woman did not suffer for her recognition of Christ as Messiah, but the man born blind was thrown out of the Temple, and the Jews sought to kill Lazarus; the Elect must understand that being chosen by God does not necessarily mean human popularity and, in a society hostile to Christian values, will mean persecution.

In addition to the three scrutinies, the presentations of the Creed and the Lord's Prayer are also celebrated to "enlighten the minds and hearts of the Elect with a deeper knowledge of Christ the Savior;" the RCIA 139 fact that the Creed and Lord's Prayer are formally *presented* to the Elect serves as a reminder that it is a *gift* of unmerited grace both to know Christ as Lord and to know God as Father. If the scrutinies inculcate purification and enlightenment by stressing how God wants to save the Elect from sin, the presentations focus on the content of His saving love. Conversion is the process of going from being able to comprehend the basic vocabulary of the language of the kingdom the Elect are entering, to actually thinking in kingdom language; having spent many months hearing the story of faith which that language comprises, at the Presentation of the Creed the Elect are ready for the Faithful to present to them the grammar by which they speak that story. This presentation gives ritual expression to the Faithful's sharing of the precious gift of revelation with which *they* have been enlightened; it is their solemn handing on of the truth that what gives structure to reality is not an impersonal code of rules to which they must scrupulously adhere, but what a personal God has done in human history—it is formed by these saving deeds that the Elect must live.

To truly know Jesus Christ as Lord is to be able to truly know God as Father; and in the Presentation of the Lord's Prayer the Faithful, having given the Elect their more formal patterns of speech in the Creed, now personalize its message by sharing with those soon to be joined to them their more familiar idiom. For several weeks the Elect have been trying to follow in the footsteps of Christ's Yes across the Lenten wilderness, and have discovered various ways they do not really want to; in presenting them with the Lord's Prayer, the Faithful are offering the Elect the prayer Christ Himself provided to help those who follow Him learn to repeat His Yes.

RCIA 147   While the Lord' Prayer (as also the Creed) can be presented earlier, if it is presented now, after the Third Scrutiny, it allows the Faithful to return to basic themes in the life of the baptized and reinforce them. For example, they can remind the Elect that when Christians pray for the coming of God's kingdom and fulfillment of His will, they are praying that they will live to be like Jesus as they were created to be, to do the Father's will as He did. The Faithful can also speak frankly of how forgiving others, letting go of wrong and loving in spite of it, can be a kind of death, but it is not optional in the Christian life. Finally, they can emphasize to the Elect that the words of the Lord's Prayer make it clear that Christians can expect that God *will* help them to overcome actual temptation and evil. In sum, the Lord's Prayer gives the Elect words for the living prayer of a son with which the Spirit of sonship will inform their lives. Now they have learned enough of how the children of God behave to pray their prayer—which, as always, includes praise of God; they are beginning to speak the special family language of those who are Church.

RCIA 35   The period of purification and enlightenment, then, is "intensely centered on conversion," which occurs as the Holy Spirit quickens the Word of God in Scripture and makes it come alive for the Elect. This can happen in the Elect's daily time of private prayer, or in interaction with members of the Faithful whose lives and relationships manifest the fruit of the Spirit, but it happens in a privileged way in the rites of public worship. The proper readings for the scrutinies and presentations thus take on a particular importance as what the Church understands God is saying to those who seek to die and rise with Christ to enable them to do so; it is as the Spirit works, through the proclamation and preaching of these readings, to change the hearts of the worshippers, that their conversion will come about. Preaching on these readings, as all catechetical preaching, is rooted in telling the story of how God has acted in relationship to humankind throughout history, so that those who hear can understand how to live in relationship with Him. Those who preach draw from the story the Scriptural personages who are examples of living faithfully with God, painting portraits of them so attractive that they function as magnets, drawing listeners who identify with them into the ongoing story of salvation. Preachers also lift up the life-giving images of Scripture like jewels, turning their many facets to the light and showing the Elect what the Faithful see in them: how these images help empower them to live the Christian life; when there are pairs of opposite images, preachers make clear what is at stake in the choice between them, urging hearers, as always, to "choose life."

Deut 30:19

It is not only through the homilies in the rites that the Spirit works through the Word to effect conversion, but also in the exorcisms of the scrutinies, where the Elect "are freed from the effects of sin and from the influence of the devil. They receive new strength in the midst of their spiritual journey and they open their hearts to receive the gifts of the Savior." Even as the exorcisms used by the Church of Jerusalem in the fourth century were considered to be effective because their words were drawn from Sacred Scripture, which was inspired by the Spirit, so the exorcisms of the RCIA scrutinies are based on the Gospel texts of those scrutinies. Many of the solemn intercessions are also inspired by Scripture.

RCIA 144
Cyril of
Jerusalem,
Procatechesis
9

Further, the power of the Word as catalyst for conversion in the liturgy is not limited to the Elect's *hearing* it spoken to them. The psalms of the rites are not simply ornaments, but work with the readings to teach the Elect to think and experience life as Christians; through the psalm antiphons the Elect learn to speak the language of faith long before they are entrusted with the Creed. By praying the psalms the Elect become part of the unfolding drama of salvation history by praying with those already in it. The psalms teach the Elect to pray by providing models for them, giving them words not only for their present condition, but for the future; in leading the Elect in Psalm 130 at the Third Scrutiny, for example, the Faithful know that after Baptism the Elect will know times of great exaltation, but perhaps also times when all seems as dry and hopeless as the Valley of Dry Bones, and when the only prayer possible is the *De Profundis.*

The rites that the Faithful provide for the Elect during this time of purification and enlightenment to help them on the last stages of their journey of prebaptismal conversion include ritual gestures as well as proclamation of the Word; while the presentation of the Creed and Lord's Prayer, signifying and effecting the handing on of the Church's faith and prayer, are the most obvious such ritual gestures, they are not the only ones. The godparents' placing of their right hands on the shoulder of the candidate they are sponsoring during the prayers of intercession, is a physical expression that the baptized life the Elect seek to enter is not simply doctrinal assent but a way of living in a faithful community, through whose prayer they are graced to be faithful. Through their formal dismissal of the Elect, the Faithful affirm to them

RCIA 153

that since it is the celebration of the Eucharist that constitutes them as Church, those in whom the gift of faith has not sufficiently matured for them to be considered Faithful are not yet capable of being part of such a celebration; yet through the blessing that accompanies this dismissal, the Faithful express their desire and prayer that the Elect soon be able to join them. By going forward and accepting the community's intercession and exorcism, the Elect publicly express their desire to change in the ways named in these prayers, and seek the grace to do so.

The expectation that the scrutinies "should complete the conversion of the Elect and deepen their resolve to hold fast to Christ and

RCIA 141

to carry out their decision to love God above all," expresses the Church's profound conviction and experience that conversion is in essence communal—*ergo* ecclesial, and since ecclesial, *ipso facto* liturgical. The rites of the period of purification and enlightenment incarnate the fact that conversion is not about individuals reordering mental concepts, but about God revealing Himself through His Word forming a People

Eucharistic
Prayer II

counted worthy to stand in His presence and serve Him. The scrutinies and presentations are appropriately celebrated during Lent, not only so that Baptism can take place at Easter, but because Lent is the season when the entire Church community together seek deeper conversion; it is expected that the rites be celebrated in such a manner that the Faith-

RCIA 146

ful as well as the Elect will benefit.

Thus, at the Rite of Election the catechumens stand before the saving God who revealed Himself in history and now reveals Himself to them, and they commit themselves, seasoned by the experience, instruction, and service of the catechumenate, to accept His call irrevocably in Baptism. During the period of purification and enlightenment they will seek a deeper conviction and understanding that the saving gospel which so attracts them is true not only conceptually, but for them personally; the readings and ritual gestures of the scrutinies and presentations are inseparable from the faith-experience of the Elect, which they both express and mediate. During the time of purification and enlightenment the Elect are seeking to grow in trust that God is who He says He is and will, according to His promise, make them who He says they are. At the Rite of Acceptance into the Order of Catechumens, the Elect left behind a life where goals, priorities, and means were determined simply by self, to journey toward a life where they are determined by God. They have since discovered that when they resisted God, insisting *they* must determine things, the "they" who resisted was not even really "them," the true selves they were created to be; now they seek to allow themselves to be ever more fully conformed to the image of Christ. Throughout their journey the Faithful have sought to help them grow in their new identity by inserting them into the story of those who have gone before them in faith. The Yes of faith that the Elect will speak at Baptism will be manifest in various ways depending on their level of maturity; while the Faithful encourage each to surrender themselves to God as fully as they can, they are adamant that the Gospel is not "try harder to earn God's gift": the very desire to choose the "Way of Life" is inspired by grace, and only by grace can the Elect receive and live it.

Didache I, 1

At the Gospel of the Rite of Election the Elect followed Christ into the desert, where they were told the bread they must live by on the Lenten journey of final preparation is the Word of God, and as they have persevered through the time of desert trial they have learned to drink Christ for their Water, see by Him as their Light, know Him as their Life; thus they have been freed to have His mind about material possessions, human esteem, and power. And increasingly they have found their thoughts turning to the One who brought them to this wilderness, who has revealed Himself more fully, the closer they come to the Paschal oasis: who will pour God's love into their hearts, who will anoint them to proclaim Jesus' Lordship, who will raise them from the dead, who will live in them and make them the heavenly Father's own children. Then they will truly be who they were created to be; there is not long to wait.

Matt 4:1

VIII. The Rites of Immediate Preparation

"The rite of recitation of the Creed prepares the elect for the profession of faith they will make immediately before they are baptized (no. 225); the rite also instructs them in their duty to proclaim the message of the Gospel" (no. 193).

"By the power of its symbolism the ephphetha rite, or rite of opening the ears and mouth, impresses on the elect their need of grace in order that they may hear the word of God and profess it for their salvation" (no. 197).

RCIA

nos. 22, 185–199,
203–205

Lectionary

John 6:35, 63-71
     (or Matt 16:13-17; see Presentation of the
     Creed)
Mark 7:31-37

Those who present themselves at this church on this date for the rites of preparation for Baptism are not here by chance. They have come knowingly to surrender themselves to a love too shockingly good to be true, except that it is. Months ago they had stumbled across the news that they were created to be totally and perfectly loved, and to reflect that love back to its Source and to all people. . . . But those were only words, then, think the Elect, attractive concepts; they had just wanted to add a nice religious dimension to their lives. When they remember what they were like then—how had they ever had the sense to start on this journey when they were so utterly ignorant of where it would take them, of what it was for? First, the beginning of the catechumenate: hearing the stories, trying to sing the songs, learning to listen and hear in prayer, and hours and hours of serving the hungry, the sick, the unwed mothers, all of them needing so much. The Christian life was about worshipping and converting, they had learned, with the former helping to effect the latter; and when they had learned enough about how to convert to sustain a lifetime of converting, they could be admitted to full membership in this pilgrim People. So they kept worshipping, they kept converting; and those who are Faithful to them as well as God kept helping them learn to pray, to obey the Holy Spirit.

And then finally came the Rite of Election, when the Faithful considered whether they were fit to compete in the Lenten trials ahead that qualify for the Paschal crown, decided that they were, and brought the Elect with them into the desert to wrestle with evil; here, the Faithful told them, they would make tough and firm their commitment to love God over all, to hold fast to Christ, whom they would come to know here as way, truth, and life of their journey. Yet even seven weeks ago, they hadn't *really* understood, hadn't known such words had so much content. But now they have emerged from the Lenten trials, both purified and enlightened. They have learned the hard way how terribly clever their Adversary is in combat, catching them off guard, stirring up sin's No in them, deceiving them into remaining in it. They have learned how to do everything they can in wielding the two-edged sword of the Word against him and, having done all, still to stand. And now, blessed are they who have passed through the time of testing, for now that they have been tried, they shall receive the crown of life.

Yet even before they are crowned with life tonight when the world is made new, there remains a final rite of preparation, heralding their joining to the kingly, priestly people. The Elect think of the One they followed into the wilderness to be tried; as His time of testing ended in His empowerment to proclaim the Gospel, so will theirs. For in this morning's rite the Elect will solemnize their transition from those who

p. 14

RCIA 4

RCIA 141

Heb 4:12
Eph 6:13
Jas 1:12

Luke 4

are hearers of the Truth to those who also confess it. As the celebrant opens the Book, the Elect focus their attention on hearing whatever last-minute instructions the Faithful would give them through the Word.

> Jesus said to them, "I am the bread of life; he who comes to me shall not hunger, and he who believes in me shall never thirst. . . . It is the spirit that gives life, the flesh is of no avail; the words that I have spoken to you are spirit and life. But there are some of you who do not believe." For Jesus knew from the first who those were that did not believe, and who it was that should betray him. And he said, "That is why I told you that no one can come to me unless it is granted him by the Father."
>
> After this many of his disciples drew back and no longer went about with him. Jesus said to the twelve, "Will you also go away?" Simon Peter answered him, "Lord, to whom shall we go? You have the words of eternal life; and we have believed, and have come to know, that you are the Holy One of God." Jesus answered them, "Did I not choose you, the twelve, and one of you is a devil?" He spoke of Judas, the son of Simon Iscariot, for he, one of the twelve, was to betray him.

John 6:35, 63-71

It is hard for the Elect not to get so caught up in the first sentence that they don't hear the rest of the reading, for they know that they *do* believe, and so tonight they shall drink of Him and never thirst, they *will* come to Him and finally know Him as bread of life and hunger no more. But they know that the Faithful would not be giving them the last-minute instructions of this reading unless they needed them, so they make themselves pay attention, listening as always for what God is saying to them about themselves and His People to whom they will so soon be irrevocably joined. They recognize themselves as those whom, with the Faithful, the Father has granted from before all time to come to His Anointed Son. The Faithful stand with them today as the faithful disciples, as Peter, those chosen by Christ who for two millennia have believed and come to know Him as Redeeming Lord. Today the Elect, long sustained on Christ's words that are spirit and life, will join Peter and the Faithful of all the ages in professing this truth.

Yet even now, so close to the font, the Elect still have a sense of being confronted by One who makes an uncompromising claim on them; Christ is not addressing them with polite words of welcome, but *challenging* them—even now: they have come to Him in this Gospel and He is asking them if they would like to leave Him! But they have been following Him so long now that they know only He has the words of eternal life—where else could they go? Then they realize that they *have* been following Him so long that they had almost gotten used to His gospel; they needed to be reminded that what they are about to profess this morning is a scandal. Being chosen by Christ may not mean what they expect: they may be rejected and unpopular, as He was. They must renew their resolve to give their lives to Him this day for *His* sake, no matter what it costs, and not for reasons of self-interest; that is why He gives them through this Gospel the opportunity to answer this question Peter and the Faithful have already answered. They must decide who He is and stake their lives on it; the faith they profess is not just a nice symbol system—the fabric of reality is based on this man being God and His Word being true. "We have believed and have come to know that you are the Holy One of God"; in a few minutes their profession of the Creed will form a mirror image of Peter's confession.

Then there is Judas—why did the Faithful include that verse? But as soon as the question comes to their minds, the Elect know the answer. Even being called and making it through the catechumenate and learning the Creed doesn't mean they are home free, or ever will be in this life. They cannot be presumptuous: even now they could still betray Him—in last-minute temptations before tonight, or even afterward; they can't be overconfident or trust in their own faithfulness. It is He who has chosen them, as He chose the Twelve and the Faithful, who knows His own who believe in Him; only in Him can they have life, so they must place all their trust in Him to make them Faithful. They cannot lose sight of this even if they want to, for looming up around them on all sides are the opposite extremes: hunger and thirst, and the bread of life; flesh and death, and spirit and life; not believing, and believing; those who draw back, and those who follow because the Father has called them; Judas' betrayal, and Peter's trust. "He spoke of Judas, the son of Simon Iscariot, for he, one of the twelve, was to betray him."

If some of the Elect were a bit pleased with themselves when they arrived this morning, somewhat more concerned about their achievement in making it so far on this journey than about the One they have been following, they are chastened now. They stand in calm expectancy as the Faithful, through the celebrant, offer them the final portion of journeybread set aside especially for them.

> Jesus returned from the region of Tyre, and went through Sidon to the Sea of Galilee, through the region of the Decapolis. And they brought to him a man who was deaf and had an impediment in his speech; and they besought him to lay his hand upon him. And taking him aside from the multitude privately, he put his fingers into his ears, and he spat and touched his tongue; and looking up to heaven, he sighed, and said to him, "Ephphetha," that is, "Be opened." And his ears were opened, his tongue was released, and he spoke plainly.

And he charged them to tell no one; but the more he charged them, the more zealously they proclaimed it. And they were astonished beyond measure, saying, "He has done all things well; he even makes the deaf hear and the dumb speak."

Mark 7:31-37

Yes, that is how it was, think the Elect. We could not hear the Word, we walked through life with no comprehension of what was truly Real; and since we were deaf to it, of course we couldn't repeat what we had never heard, we could speak nothing of Reality. But somehow the Faithful got us to go with them to Jesus, and they begged Him (*how* they have begged him, these many months, through all their intercession!) to heal us. And this Jesus didn't make a spectacle of us, waving His arms around while others were entertained at our expense. He took us aside and ministered to us one at a time, and He seemed genuinely grieved at our affliction. When He touched us, we could hear His Word and we knew who He was, and for the first time in our life we could speak Truth, speak that language which alone is truly speech. Yes, that is how it was, and none of it was our own doing: it was His gift that the Faithful came to us, His gift that we now hear and speak. And we have come to consummate His gift, by enacting with our bodies what He has gifted in our hearts. "And they were astonished beyond measure, saying, 'He has done all things well; He even makes the deaf hear and the dumb speak.'" The celebrant finishes his explanation and beckons the Elect to come before him.

RCIA 198, 199

"Ephphetha: that is, be opened, that you may profess the faith you hear, to the praise and glory of God."

RCIA 56

At the rite that set the Elect on this journey, Christ through His Body, the Church, signed their ears with His Cross so that they could hear His voice; as Christ's Body the Faithful have opened the ears of the Elect, freed their tongues, and given them the Word to speak. Now, with this Ephphetha Rite and one last prayer of intercession, the Faithful bring this task to its completion.

RCIA 195

"Lord, we pray for these Elect . . ." As the celebrant stretches out his hands the Faithful think of the Gospel of the deaf man's healing, just proclaimed, as a glorious sound from heaven; as each of the Elect recite the Creed they will be an echo of that Gospel.

". . . As they profess their belief with their lips, may they have faith in their hearts and accomplish your will in their lives. . ." Back at that first rite the Elect had figured that sooner or later there would be a bunch of things they'd have to memorize and then be able to pass a written test. But the "test" they dreaded is already over, they suddenly realize. For them to stand before the Faithful and profess the Creed this morning is not to have to perform for them in an alien language;

for by the time this day has come, their recitation is for them simply a matter of saying what is most important to them in the language they have come to think and speak in as their own. They remember how they had felt their desire to speak their Yes to God with their lives, but how it had needed form and shape. The Faithful had handed on to them the truths that form their Yes, just as *they* had received those truths; today the Elect will begin to do the same. They recall how the Faithful have told them that the Christian life requires an ever-deeper assent to the Triune God who is Love, an ever-deeper realization of the Truth, and reflect that the rites by which they have been prepared have done the same: from accepting Christ as Living Water, Light, and then Life, to being willing to proclaim Him before all. To begin as a catechumen was to be a disciple, to listen, to set out on a journey; to be an Elect catechumen was to learn not only to listen, but to commit oneself to obey in a radical way, to sell all for the one Pearl, and to take the journey they began with Abram even to its end, the Cross. ". . . through Christ our Lord." "Amen."

Matt
13:45-46

Heb 12:1

And so each one steps forward to join the cloud of witnesses who some five weeks ago came to present to them the crown in which the Church of the ages keeps the precious gift of faith in Jesus Christ; as the Elect have memorized the words they will profess, their understanding of them has deepened. "We believe in one God . . ." This is not a list of what *we* have done, think the Elect, that we recite to show our qualifications; this is what God has done in our midst.

RCIA 196

". . . We believe in one Lord, Jesus Christ . . ." It is the Spirit-charged Word that has opened their ears, and freed their tongues, to speak these words; who first kindled faith's flame in them and, now, as they proclaim each truth, emblazons it in them as fact, as Truth by which all other truths are measured. As the Elect hear their own voices proclaim the redeeming Lordship of Christ, they wonder at what is happening: it was a statement before, we said it with all piety, now it is a fire that consumes us.

". . . We believe in the Holy Spirit . . ." These things are all self-evident to God, think the Elect; we see them, know them, through faith—but faith is knowledge too, they see.

". . . We acknowledge one baptism for the forgiveness of sins . . ." Tonight they will take the desire to be as gods that their first parents bequeathed to them, to the font to be drowned; too long have they been locked in mortal combat with their No.

". . . We look for the resurrection of the dead and the life of the world to come . . ." All the promises of God find their Yes in Him: "I *am* the Yes," He says. "Amen."

2 Cor 1:20

Rev 3:14

In the deep silence the Faithful exchange significant glances: "He has done all thing well." Once more they have cause to join their forebears in the Gospel, proclaiming Christ as healer and blessing Him for it; the newly baptized will not be the only ones celebrating after the Vigil tonight. But there are yet hours of quiet waiting, hours of stomachs rumbling from the fast; and the Faithful, ever hospitable, have one last blessing and dismissal.

RCIA 204   The Elect feel their heartbeats begin to slow down, and in relief they soak in the words of the blessing; it goes by too quickly. ". . . May the Lord be with you until we gather again to celebrate His paschal mystery." "Amen;" for one last time, as Elect, they depart. But this time, they know, they have not been dismissed from a liturgy they cannot consummate, but *into* the next part of the liturgy: into the black void before the beginning of the world and the spark of life where everything begins. That is still some hours away, but what are hours compared to the months they have journeyed to get here? Tonight they will pass through font and flame and step into the strong embrace of the One who trampled down death by death. Until then they wait, wait with the Faithful, who wait with Christ, in the tomb.

Liturgy of Good Friday, Gospel

The time of the catechumenate has come to an end. For months the catechumens had told people, "I am converting"; now they have come through the odd land of the present progressive tense and are finally ready to cross the threshold into the household of faith. Accepting the invitation extended to them perhaps years before at the Rite of Acceptance into the Order of Catechumens, they have seen where Jesus was staying; with Jesus, they have been with the wild beasts—and angels have ministered to them. The Scripture lessons of the rites have articulated the terrain of their journey in faith, and have been their journeybread throughout the catechumenate. And the shadowlands of the catechumenate have prepared them well for the shadowlands of the Church, where the kingdom is always here, and always just out of sight.